SPRING TO MIND

ZOË COPLEY

SPRING TO MIND

Matador
5 Weir Road
Kibworth Beauchamp
Leicester LE8 0LQ, UK
Tel: (+44) 116 279 2277
Email: books@troubador.co.uk
Web: www.troubador.co.uk/matador

In this work, any resemblance to a person, government department, firm, business or
school is probably pure coincidence.

ISBN 978 1848761 681

British Library Cataloguing in Publication Data.
A catalogue record for this book is available from the British Library.

Typeset in 11pt Bembo by Troubador Publishing Ltd, Leicester, UK

Printed in Great Britain by the MPG Books Group, Bodmin and King's Lynn

Matador is an imprint of Troubador Publishing Ltd

In memory of my mother -
an optimist and an inspiration.

FOREWORD
Vive ut vivas

Over the past several years, hundreds of self-help and popular psychology books have been published promising the "Answer" - the secret to finding happiness and meaning. We are told why we are as we are, advised on how to get what we want and equipped with techniques and skills to aid us on this quest. The reader clamours for more, the publishers keep printing, the shelves heave under the weight of all that wisdom.

Hence, this book. But *Spring to Mind* is also a personal story. A story of a journey from confusion and frustration towards clarity and fulfilment; from dislocation towards congruence.

The catalyst for this journey was coaching and the immense learning it can bring about. Coaching involves a client being truly listened to, challenged and questioned, always with their goals and outcomes in mind. The process of becoming a coach and the many hours of coaching I received during it, proved to be transformative. While it sounds clichéd, coaching helped me to rediscover my voice.

So while this book is a snapshot of one journey, many elements of it transcend the individual. The underlying themes and motivations are universal and timeless. The desire to make a difference, the need to be heard, the quest for happiness and meaning, the search for ways of coping in stressful times, the ambition to be "successful".

I would like to promise that by reading this book you will find the "Answer".

But you won't, because it doesn't lie in any book, any course, any website or any other person. It lies within you. And it's good at hiding. It knows all the best haunts in among the insecurities and self doubt, the family expectations, the regrets, the disappointed longings and the "shoulds". But it is in there and searching it out is made easier by coaching. Why? Because with coaching, the learning, the journey and the decisions are yours alone. Coaching provides no advice, no quick fixes, no theory or therapy. Based in the belief that you are expert on you, it requires that you work out what you are seeking and commit to finding it.

This is not to suggest that coaching is the "Answer". It is but one tool. There are, of course, a myriad of others; all freely available too. A sense of humour and perspective, a positive mindset, faith.... A lot of coffee.

Finally, *Spring to Mind* is a challenge – to lighten up, to find the humour in the humdrum and the originality in the ordinary, to believe in the possibilities, to look within for the source of meaning. And ultimately, to live as you would dare to live.

From the moment I picked up your book until I laid it down, I was convulsed with laughter. Some day I intend reading it.
Groucho Marx

An optimist is the human personification of spring.
Susan J. Bissonette

5 February, 2009

Dear Mummy,

Please find enclosed a succession of letters that I have been writing to you over the past few months since we returned from Australia and learnt that you have leukaemia.

As my early letters set out, my intent was to reach out to you in the uncertain and worrying times you faced. Ironically, the mere process of writing proved therapeutic and cathartic, and as a result most of these letters have stayed, unprinted, on my laptop until now. While the initial motivation for writing was a desire to connect with you and Dad, the impetus became a need to identify with the humour and humanity of the circumstances.

My letters were intended to entertain you or distract you from chemotherapy and treatment. I have done no such thing and I have offered very little in the way of meaningful support. Once again, it is you and Dad who have been the rock for the rest of us; brave and strong and uncomplaining in every moment of the past few months. You are both truly inspirational.

While these letters began as a conduit to you, they became a direct line for me to myself. You may well pooh-pooh this notion as self-help nonsense and psycho-babble. But ultimately, your illness and my career change from law to coaching has helped me to rediscover my voice. I now believe that something of what I can express might be of interest to others. Hopefully, in any case, my words may still resonate with you.

Accordingly, and in the hope that nothing you read in the

attached bundle will occasion you anything other than a laugh, a nod, a smile, and only an occasional eye roll, I hope to put my musings to a wider use. So, could I ask you to do me the honour of reading these pages as my first literary critic?

I hasten to add that given my overt criticism of the fourth estate herein, yours may be the only unbiased review I can count on, so make the most of this opportunity.

All my love and undying respect,

Tess

18 September, 2008

Dear Claire,

Thank you for your lovely and thoughtful birthday card. I was touched that you found time to send it given recent events with Mum. Are you all on tenterhooks wondering which of the many side effects may be the first to manifest itself and whether the drugs will rid her of this cancer?

Are you generally optimistic? Part of me is probably in denial that this is as serious as it really may be, as I am feeling so certain that she will respond well to the treatment and achieve a remission. It all seems somehow unreal.

It is almost exactly 11 years ago since her first cancer scare and I remember being gripped with a strange panic. It took quite a concentrated and conscious effort to adjust to the news and process what it might mean. While, like you, I had been away from Brisbane for a few years by then, I had not ever really contemplated Mum and Dad's health in that way; namely that they could be dangerously ill with me living 12,000 miles away. I remember it was a late September Saturday afternoon and I was just back from a fortnight's holiday in New York when I felt an overwhelming need to sit on the ground, not the floor, but actual turf. So I spent hours on the grass in the communal gardens opposite my flat - taking courage and fortitude from Mother Earth.

Since hearing of the diagnosis of leukaemia last week I have not had a chance to do the same. Maybe all that sitting on the ground in 1997 was rather a good thing and keeps me connected even now. Maybe you can prepare for these things in a sort of way – at least this time the shock is not so great. Maybe it's just that I haven't seen a speck of dry earth for several days. Also I know that after such a long time since that first scare and in light of all the weird auto immune illnesses she has fought and lived with, one cannot help but feel blindly optimistic that she will triumph yet again.

Polyarteritis nodosa, BOOP (Bronchiolitis obliterans organising pneumonia), myelodysplasia and the hospitalisations for the various complications along the way. Now leukaemia... But you know, she will probably outlive us all...

In any case, you and all the family are in my thoughts and prayers and I wish I was there. Mum could not have asked for a more loving, devoted and generous daughter, Claire. You will be a great support to us all.

On a lighter note, I have decided to write to Mum with lots of chatty upbeat letters to alleviate the suffering of hair loss and nausea and oesophageal blisters. Initially I thought I would send her some British magazines – always a great source of escapist pleasure. *Country Living* or *Homes and Gardens*. But then I thought better of it. Even more than *In Style* or *Vogue* or that dreaded *Tattler*, which depresses the hell out of me, they might just remind her, lying in that cancer ward wondering if she will ever smell a flower again, let alone walk in the country, that all is not a rosy garden in Kent with a classy architect couple and children called Polly and Percy, or capable of fixing with the purchase of a new conservatory, an AGA or Boden's new season's Mac in green. Mind you, I could do with a new Mac.

So while I cannot be physically close at this time, I will try to be connected by mail. If I can cheer her up, or lighten her load, it will be some consolation perhaps. Maybe all I am really trying to do is maintain a connection across this distance.

So Claire, prepare her for the onslaught of mail coming her way. It will be reminiscent of the early months I spent at Cambridge when my lengthy epistles distracted me from the eternal grey of the skies, my complete lack of friends, the college diet of potatoes done eight ways, the parlous state of my finances and the realisation that *Chariots of Fire* had largely been filmed elsewhere.

Send all of our love to Mum and Dad. Don't work too hard.

Tessie x

19 September, 2008

Dear Mum,

I am not sure yet how you are feeling today, as it is too early to call you there. You are probably eating some sort of hospital gruel or cold cardboard and reading the newspaper. In any case, I am writing to you to cheer you up a little. You are now my captive audience, given that you are not yet discharged and recuperating at home, but stuck there in bed and too ill to read a heavy novel or even a fashion rag. You can have a big bellyache to me if you need to, when I call.

I realised after I finished the coaching course in July just how much I enjoy writing. On the course my observations seemed to strike a chord and amuse my colleagues. I had a sense that my own light had been switched back on. Finally, after all these years as a fish out of water during which I subconsciously quelled my personality, it seemed I could speak aloud once more. But absent a course, a stand up comedy act, a new career in party entertainment or signing up with Toastmasters, I had nowhere to channel my thoughts; so I started to write.

For a long time I have felt that I have a book in me. I have flirted with the idea of a modern classic. For years I have secretly harboured a jealous resentment of friends and acquaintances who are "writers". Over the past few months I have been recording my thoughts in a haphazard way; even from time to time copying Agent McGee on *NCIS* and "free/flow writing" to just "get it down" – to uncover some subconscious or long buried knowledge. I know that I am not alone in this pursuit. Doesn't everyone have "write a book" on their list?

More recently I have wanted to explore the great themes of the human experience. Not love, life, death. The more immediate and urgent ones - tedium, mediocrity, striving, disappointment, calorie counting, naval gazing, domestic envy and middle class angst. While I have felt that there is so much to say, I could not put pen to paper. So much of what I thought or felt about these great themes was neither original nor interesting. I could amuse myself perhaps, but how was I to make a story out of striving mediocrity? How could I plot an interesting narrative around the banalities of raising children, shopping for groceries, and going to work? After all, we live and breathe this every day. It's not that it is unpalatable; merely obvious, irritating.

So, I want to write. Yet, I should walk before I run. I can, therefore, "just get it down". So the fact that you are too ill to spend long sessions on the phone listening and chatting brings me an opportunity to write to you (you see – it's all about me). Instead of the instant gratification of hearing your melodious tones in my ear, I can indulge this creative and expressive urge, while also clarifying my thinking and enjoying a self indulgent giggle, just as if we were having a conversation. In addition, with my impressions of your advice and musings ringing in my head, there is no chance of writer's block striking. So we can't have our regular chats, but we can still be in touch. Perhaps in addressing the themes I mention above as I experience them – namely, the search for meaning in the ordinary and the routine - I will unlock some heretofore dormant creative spark and find that I *do* have that novel in me after all.

So where is this preoccupation with life's great mysteries coming from? Well I have been noticing the trend to glorify the mediocre and venerate celebrity for its own sake, a lot lately. In our schools, the halls of power, in our newspapers and magazines, the average is hailed in superlatives. Children are trained to expect a reward just for showing up. In the commercial world bonuses are paid despite failure and disgrace. I am not suggesting that mediocrity is acceptable across the board. Indeed, in the realms of sport and scientific endeavour, mediocrity will certainly not suffice. But I am noticing what I am noticing. And it seems that all too often it is the sensational or marketable or celebrity sponsored item that catches the public imagination. It seems that mass productions and dumbing down is taking away much of the challenge and originality that used to be a defining feature of British life. For example, are we so lacking in imagination and aspiration as to be truly entertained by 12 not particularly good looking and basically uninteresting people cohabiting in a house or, God forbid, a subtropical jungle, picking fights with each other for six weeks? Is the cellulite quotient on the butts of glamorous Hollywood starlets more important than presidential elections, economic crises and famine? No, just far more sensational and entertaining, of course. Oh and even *flabby* bottoms sell more papers than emaciated ones on small people in developing countries.

Perhaps it is merely that I am noticing these things because I am not exerting myself to seek out challenge and provocation. When I first came to the UK I spent most days listening to Radio 4, reading newspapers and talking to students. Now, I consider a night at the cinema in front of a popular Rom-Com a treat... But that does not invalidate my concern. Because if I cannot easily access stimulation or elevation, mustn't the same be true of huge swathes of the population?

The second reason for my wanting to reflect on the issues faced by those in the "middle lane" is that they are universal and sometimes, soul-destroying. I wonder if they will become more so in times of economic down turn, recession and increased unemployment. I am referring to the small irritations and daily struggles and challenges, that are not unusual or extreme, but which are common to everyone. Understand Mum, I am not talking about fighting cancer, living with a severe disability, or in abject poverty.

Not struggling with serious addiction, prolonged abuse, chronic unemployment or the aftermaths of a tsunami. Thankfully.

No, I am talking about the small things which in and of themselves are to quote you: "neither here nor there". The minor trials and upsets, the quotidian dilemmas. We are plagued by questions such as what to wear to the school assembly (or how not to compete with the French mothers who are so chic and always wear shoes one should not be walking in), how to avoid the office bore at the Christmas party, how to get the coffee you want first time, how to carry the dry cleaning home over the pushchair handles and not have it drag in the gutter, how to get your husband to carry the dry cleaning home and not lose your favourite dress on the way, how to keep shirts really white, how to make breakfast more appetising, how to stay awake through tedious dinner repartee... oh and how to get six years of greasy hand marks off the wall by the stairs without stripping the paintwork.

These little burdens, together with the slights and the disappointments of years of work, family relationships, friendships and the stress of navigating life in the big city, cumulatively grind you down, leaving you aching, cold and alone, a shadow of your best self. What happens to the joy, humour, spontaneity and sense of purpose? Can intelligence, high emotional quotient, good looks or pots of money be enough to defend one against this assault from without and within?

The spirit is indomitable, I know. The day spas, the boutiques, the wine bars, the therapists' offices and the football stadia are filled with the hopeful. There is still a glimmer of optimism. You can see it at the designer clearance sales and in the queues for lottery tickets. I want that glimmer to grow and burn bright and strong. I want all of those hopeful people and the ones who have no hope, to feel and see the good within the trying, the humour within the tragic and the beauty within the dross. I think that is what I need to say.

But enough of me and these musings. I will be wearing you out.

Dear Mum, lots of love to you and Dad. Big hugs from the boys (who still want me to ask Dad for his definition of "Galute" by the way). They are wondering whether the resident scrub turkey is still vexing Granddad with its habitual dragging of leaves across his lawn.

Tess x

20 September, 2008

Dear Mum,

I hope you are feeling a little better. In response to your question about my urge to write, the answer is that I feel that I have something to say. I daresay, like chocolate and coffee, this desire to speak and be heard is just a new addiction to feed; a yearning for attention, a longing for the spotlight that comes with the well timed and witty rejoinder across the seminar room on a coaching course. If it is an addiction, I just hope it is a cheaper one. By the time I add up the weekly cost of the skinny extra dry cappuccinos (with free dark Belgian chocolate) to go, the extra Underground trip to and from the best coffee shop in the city (sometimes twice daily), the Green and Black Organic Pralines and the Coco Pops Mega Munchers cereal for late night snacking, I could pay for the coaching course all over again. Still, cheaper than a life coach!

It did occur to me – in jest - that I should commit my thoughts to a blog. Are you thinking: "what's a blog?" If you are – it's an on-line/internet published diary or journal or place to share one's thoughts. You can give certain people rights of access so they can read, respond, open a dialogue.

But I couldn't do it. Not only does the technology baffle me, but also the idea that I too could become an internet-age-navel-gazing-live-in-and-through-the-eyes-of-my-two-on-line-mates-and-thus-feel-validated-loser, fundamentally too lazy and self absorbed to call a friend for a chat, terrified me. Did I really have nothing better to do with my time? I can hear you tsking: "You have three small children, a job and a travelling husband; don't you have enough to do?"

Blogs are a valid form of social and creative articulation. Perhaps in 300 years they will be revered and cherished and valued just as we value the diary of Samuel Pepys. Indeed there are so many informative blogs and postings shedding light on all sorts of topics and providing wonderful resources for research and inquiry, that avoiding them entirely is both impossible and naive. Like the Pamphlets of yesteryear or the village newspaper, they are a rich reflection of the thinking of the day.

So where was I? To blog or not to blog. No, despite their value, I could never blog. So, what else could I do? Keep a journal? Mmm. It could just be an indulgent diatribe full of my banal thoughts and petty observations for the general amusement of no one at all. A waste of time and just something else to delete from my laptop when the memory runs out. Or more likely, a source of great angst and stress when the children in their never ending search for internet pictures of planes and Sugababes accidentally erase it, thus prompting one of those mellifluous lecture series I so love to deliver and they so love to hear.

So, that's why I am writing to you. I will conduct a long, more or less one-sided conversation with you. My thoughts are not highbrow, nor sensationalist, not even literary. While a part of me dreams that one day I will write something capable of easy serialisation and conversion to a screen play, my primary purpose now is to reach out to you. When you are safely back home and I finish writing because we will be speaking so often once more, we will have an anthology of sorts, full of insights into the boring and the trying; "A Diary of Everybody" or "One woman's search for meaning in the Weetabix and the washing". You would never buy such a book, Mum, but packaged as letters from your daughter you might enjoy the knowledge – let's not flatter to deceive that it amounts to wisdom – I have accumulated during this time in the UK ("I thought I detected a faint accent – are you an Antipodean?"). I won't labour the most boring bits – the housework, the battle for good childcare, or the juggle of work and home life, indeed working life generally. Topics that bear no further elucidation but which are so universally relevant and so unfailingly tedious as to guarantee some sympathy, even from the older generation. In your day after all, children were not in childcare, nor running around town to coffee shops, and most mothers were not having *careers*. Nevertheless, we can all identify with and share in the joys of family life and the incredible depth of humour and feeling that surrounds so much of it. Is that not worth writing home about?

So while I would like to pen something erudite and broadening, I suspect that in the final analysis that will have to await something more. If not my longed for trek to Antarctica, the successful establishment of my nascent coaching practice, or a bit more "felt life", then perhaps another course - creative writing, say...

So I have found my voice but what to say... In an averagely humdrum existence in central London in which everything I do, think or feel, has at some level been said or done before, it still strikes me just how often I bite my tongue. I self censor and keep my thoughts to myself. How many times have we been talking and you have said to me "next time you should say..." or "what you should have said was..."? Too many. It is time I gave myself permission to just bloody well say what I think then and there, in the moment, every time, not just selectively or occasionally or after a really good day on a course. If I do nothing more in these rants to you than practise doing just that, then I will have spent my time well.

I had better sign off now; it's late and you must be exhausted!

Much love and well wishes,

Tx

15

21 September, 2008

Dear Mum,

I was delighted to hear that Janet from your bridge club visited you and regaled you with the gossip and recent winning plays. How are the various new romances and pairings progressing? If Andrew should predecease me I am definitely joining your club for my second go round. It must be a great distraction from your blood pressure and swollen feet. I was delighted to hear that Rob is considering doing a course to train as an executive coach. I am very happy to give him the low-down on my course, as Janet requested. I had such a transformational and confidence building time "becoming a coach", as you know. I am quite evangelical even now.

Rather than bore *you* with the details again – much of which I can no longer remember in my haste to reinvent myself – I will enclose a note for Rob setting out some "Hints and Tips" that more or less sum up my experience on the course. It is probably too soon for me to comment on the actual process of starting a business as a coach. I *want* to be able to provide meaningful insights into how to keep up the momentum after the ring binder is closed for the last time, the babysitter is paid and the niggling doubt as to whether it was really worth it (not just the - God, where is the pound sign on the damn yankee computer – 4000 pounds sterling in tuition fees – who knows what in coffee, phone bills and broadband time surfing the web for a business name that rings true and a business card design that will not stimulate nor bore the recipient too much) have set in. I don't actually have any such wisdom, apart from the obvious: make sure the day job is trying and poorly paid.

Tell Janet that Rob is welcome to call if he wants further or better particulars. You can pass the enclosed letter on to Janet when she next visits. I hope that the bridge piece from the *Times* enclosed isn't too easy for you.

Thinking of you. The boys are writing separately and busily drawing pictures for you as I type. Tommy is keen to share his depiction of a "hippopopinous". Jack has designed a new fighter jet – three winged – and Felix is assiduously converting his copy thereof into a boat before Jack notices the offensive plagiarism.

T x

21 September, 2008

Dear Rob,

Good to hear you are thinking of a new career. I was surprised to learn through your mother that you had tired of plumbing, especially since you had such a great life doing all the landscaping work as well. Still, the drought can't have helped. I have set out some thoughts about coaching training below. I gather that you want to hear about how I got into it given that last time we spoke I was on my way to Cambridge to do my Masters of Law. The short version is that after spending 14 years practising law I needed a more flexible career, where I could work with "real" people with "real" problems. The longer version follows.

Where to start – ok – I will set the scene. As the mother of three young sons, my husband working abroad and coming home every couple of weekends, I was burnt out and bored by my career as a lawyer. I was working part time (in fact I still am but I moved into the Government Legal Service around the same time as I started the course), having the work life balance sussed (i.e. I got paid for showing up and doing a bit of work no one else wanted to do and my employer got to win awards for being flexible and family friendly) but I felt boxed in, underutilised and resentful that my time away from the children was not being spent meaningfully. I craved a people oriented outlet. I wanted to draw on my legal acumen and my strengths in analysis, and communication but in a new milieu where I could somehow make the world a better place (and still get paid). As a lawyer I felt fungible and dispensable. I knew that working part time in private practice would secure me no pay rises or promotions. I was frustrated and lost.

More than that though, I was eager to leave some sort of legacy. Perhaps having children focuses the mind on what sort of contribution one is making to society. As a tax lawyer I saw that I had probably done more ill than good – helping companies save millions of pounds in tax. Admittedly, I can lay claim to the honour of being instrumental in introducing tables and flowcharts to the UK legislative arena when I drafted the Capital Allowances rewrite in 1997-98, before I left the civil service. A high point, I admit, especially since the lead parliamentary counsel on the tax law rewrite project at the time had assured me such devices to aid readability would not in fact find their way into actual legislation; such outlandish, modern gimmicks being beyond the scope of the UK taxpayer, professional adviser or courts to interpret. Imagine my delight when 4 years later I stumbled upon my very own words enacted in the Capital Allowances Act 2001 reprinted in the *Butterworths Yellow Tax Handbook* (a weighty phone book of a tome full of tax law and amendments) and indeed set out in the form of a table - a *box* - if you will! The irony and triumph was sweet.

They say motherhood is the great leveller, the most important job you will ever have, the source of great joy and pain and so on. What they don't say is that by having more children and securing 12 months maternity leave, no questions asked (about the leave, that is – the things they do ask blows the mind e.g. the boss inquiring about my breast feeding ambitions in a packed elevator of male colleagues with an average age of 26, the senior manager commenting on my girth on his way back from the gents in front of at least 5 workmates, the secretaries asking whether I was expecting triplets – you get the idea), one can safely delay the inevitable decision about finding a career more to one's liking. I had three fabulous boys though, so crunch time had come when number three at the age of 15 months was still waking for his bottle twice a night and no amount of reasoning (which one can in fact do quite well with a 15 month old) would alter the fact that I was still looking like the mother of a 15 day old and still trudging to my go nowhere job in tax advice (euphemistically so-called – the more savvy know how much "advice" those city big shots provide and how much is pure invention and speculation). I was yearning for the luxury of a more fulfilling job outside the home.

You may remember from our university days that I had plans to "change the world". More latterly it involved doing so literally, by saving the planet from global warming. I had stood up to Mum when she said: "Give that one away, love, there are smart people working on it". I had flirted with the idea of retraining as a water law specialist. As a landscaping plumber working through a drought you will need no persuading that such would be a worthwhile and challenging role. I had excitedly amassed a large pile of prospectuses for university degrees in environmental science and environmental policy. And yet I felt defeated at the same time. This was an overwhelming challenge beyond my control and influence. No course could persuade me otherwise. Every edition of *The Ecologist* further depressed my hopes for the generations to come. And my dejection only deepened each Tuesday and Friday as I watched with frustration as the rubbish collectors threw my carefully separated recyclables in with general trash yet again. Can you imagine my despair at the sight of the queues outside Topshop and Primark for another armload of disposable fashion to help brighten those landfill dioramas next season? What was I to do?

And remember how I had plans to help people? At one time I thought creating clear and simple laws would help people. I soon gave up on that and planned the eco friendly supper club that doubled as a homeless drop in centre by day. I lost sight of that dream after several disbelieving looks from work colleagues. Then I had the demoralised years during which I tried to convince myself that having a couple of good friends was enough.

Finally, after having children I began to see that there might be value in helping people to be happy and to keep perspective; to see the good things in their lives, the humour and joy that children can bring. In spite of the newfound purpose, I too was one of those short tempered harassed looking office workers pouring out of the underground, tsking at the bottleneck at the turnstiles at Blackfriars at 9.30am every Monday, Tuesday and Thursday (flexible working days), lamenting my lack of sleep and general disarray. I knew in my heart that the clock was ticking and if I did not find an alternate (flexible) career with heart, I would indeed be working towards a fourth baby come Christmas.

And then wham! I met a Coach on a networking course. Ostensibly I was there to learn how to introduce myself to strangers and mention my firm in the opening gambit. What actually happened was that I discovered the answer. It all finally made sense.

All the personal development programmes I had participated in during the heady years of middle management – trying to raise my powers of influence, enhance my potential leadership skills, learn how to delegate - in countless country house hotels designed for the very purpose of confusing the course attendees after a late night in the bar. All those "Apprentice" style treasure hunts and mock client presentations with groups of not-at-all similarly placed middle managers. I had loved those courses and longed to be the facilitators who just "got" everyone so well and were so great at making the programme fun and memorable. For a time between baby one and baby two I was owed a few courses and I was so good at the stuff they targeted in terms of developing "soft" skills that I just wanted to do courses for a living. The feedback and the learning was very intense and gratifying. For three days every six months or so I actually felt like a functioning professional instead of the fraud and dud I usually regarded myself as in the office. I was the best candidate. I won the prizes and I revelled in the knowledge that I was not actually stupid after all. I could do these tasks well and most importantly, influentially. I could not only think laterally, solve problems and impress the facilitators, but I could also work with people effectively.

The high point was probably the dragon boating episode on Lake Windermere where I single-handedly secured a clue from a raft cast adrift in the middle of the water, rescued some team mates and capsized the opposition canoe; all the while strategising about the next clue, second guessing the task itself (convinced there was a trick in the brief) and managing by walkie-talkie the now disparate land-based members of my team who had lost heart. I was 26 weeks preggers at the time. What I lacked in physical tone I certainly made up for in my mental agility, my ingenuity, my can-do attitude and my sheer commitment.

So yes – coaching – I was all ears to the news that one could make a living running courses, listening to people and helping them transform their lives. I could do this, I thought. And finally the tenacity I displayed on those courses and in sending back all those poorly made lattes masquerading as dry cappuccinos, in arranging my wedding across 12,000 miles and in bearing and raising three kids with near family no closer than said 12,000 miles had another use. I was googling and calling coaching organisations to find a course, learn how to do it, price it, sell it... and ...

Six months later I was enrolled and ready to go. I had found the Course.

And so the other plans went on the back burner; somewhere between the baked on lentils and the crusty burnt Illy coffee stain, but in front of the spurted tomato juice on the wall (organic tinned, chopped in own juice from Waitrose). What of the plan to save the planet? I let it go.

And what of the plan to help people? By golly by jingo – it looked as it if it might just come off. Perhaps through coaching I could help people meet their potential and find meaning and fulfilment in their lives. Maybe I could start bundling up those oversized knickers and maternity swimmers for Oxfam!

Rob, the Course was like crumbs to a starving man. I was mesmerised by the idea that I would find a fulfilling profession. Maybe I could hold my head high when my son asked me, "how was your day at that job that takes you away from us?"

Turning to the nature of the Course itself, I should say that mine was run over several months but I think what I learnt about courses can be applied more generally. Accordingly, this account is not too specific but hopefully will provide valuable insights into self help and personal development courses that run in a modular way across an extended period. The Course was very professionally run and attracted very experienced and discerning participants. It was not in the least bit airy fairy or new agey or radical. It wasn't political nor technically complex. It was intelligent and thought provoking, engaging and structured.

I cannot therefore provide much insight into courses of a different bent – e.g. the crazy, the Out There, the con jobs, the break-you-down-to-build-you-back-up secret agenda ones. I am not sure what appeals to you, but if you want the more business or executive type client then steer clear of the cultish ones, or anything that advertises its qualifications using crystals, chakras or too many pastel colours. Also, be mindful that even *with* a great training programme that could help you set up a business, gain greater self awareness and launch you into a new career, there is still the step change in how you market yourself, change direction and indeed, see yourself in the new role as coach.

While I firmly believe in the value of coaching and I now believe I can do it well, I still have gone through a surprisingly difficult process over several months of letting go of the former identity as a lawyer. Indeed I am still not free of that persona yet, as

I retain the part time job in a tax law advisory role even now. This may not be an issue for you. Maybe the plumber turned coach will ring true very quickly. In my case I underestimated the depth and extent to which I felt invested in my self-image as a lawyer.

For years I had nurtured the notion that I was some sort of Ally McBeal (thin and quirky, not neurotic), Judge John Deed (interesting cases, maverick), Mary Tyler Moore (stylish and independent) career woman, all because I had a dusty and no doubt rusty university medal, three prizes in law, a moot competition winner's trophy, 10 years debating and adjudicating experience, the letters LLM (Cantab) after my name, and goodness knows how many solicitors and barristers in the family. Who was I to throw it all away?

And yet what truly ensures success in the practice of tax law in London? Not academic merit, or integrity, love of language and communication or a belief in the goodness of my fellow man. No – I tell you – a Masters from Cambridge?! What use was any of that to me during those wilderness years in the City? What had I been thinking? I should have found a course that would teach me to overcome my total lack of political will, to show me how to appear to know (and care) about football and the names of obscure and obsolete Court of Appeal cases. I needed a programme to teach me how to conceal that my brain starts to atrophy at the mere suggestion that I consider the accounting treatment of complex tax structured finance deals. If only I had learnt the cure for preferring the gym to lunch in the staff canteen, and the company of my kids and the cast of the *West Wing* to that of my work mates. If I was to make it big as a tax lawyer I needed to turn down an early night in with a good crime thriller and stay in the office, being seen to be the last to leave or at the very least being available to join the others going out to a wine bar or pub for a lager or a glass of pinot (dahling!). If I was to be judged "meets expectations" in annual performance reviews, I had to know how to find answers to difficult and impenetrable tax queries while appearing to already know. And, above all, I had to do this with a flick of my bouncy hair, a coy yet coquettish smile and a little bit of leg showing. Oh - I almost forgot – I absolutely required training in knowing when to shut my mouth and merely nod and giggle at the partners' misogynistic jokes and self serving war stories.

In short, I was just not cut out for private practice. It took a while to accept this and not regard myself as a failure. And yet the good bits of the legal training I bring with me. Once a lawyer... Moreover, one does not throw the baby out with the bathwater. Mind you, sometimes one does slip and injure ones head, back and hip when the no longer small baby (little bugger) throws said water all over the floor, causing one to wish one had had a little more prescience when one had the chance...

Finally though, I made the leap of faith. By the end of the first day of the Course, with Andrew back in London bonding with his sons for the duration, I recognised that I could do this listening and analysing and clarifying thing. Crikey, the better part of my life had been spent doing just those things. What better use for the skills of a failed lawyer who actually likes people?

So Rob, if you are still interested in knowing more about the Course itself then I can share a few tips. I gather that you might be coming to the UK to see your sister and so are considering programmes run here. Heavens, if you want hints on life in the UK, I am happy to oblige, but that will require another missive altogether. Focussing on just attending courses, I would say, and this may sound trite, there is a lot to be said for being well prepared and for managing the subtle and unspoken elements of interaction with others. I don't say this lightly, actually. It might seem second nature to you as a plumber. You get along with people, especially women of a certain age, given the role you play in their bathrooms and laundries.

However, on courses, there can be so much going on in the room – personality clashes, anger management issues, emotion and tears, facilitators' in-fighting and sometimes even a lot of romance, not to mention some tragic wardrobe debacles. As a course attendee one does owe a huge debt of gratitude to all of those people who did a trial make-up and hair-do before each module and managed to coordinate dress and shoes. They deserve recognition for the joy they brought to the rest of the group. I know that you will understand this Rob. Your sartorial elegance and attention to detail are vivid in my mind's eye when I reflect on our days as undergrads. Your efforts were bold and accomplished.

In this area I apologise in advance if my tone is a bit directive. I do not lay claim to any greater knowledge than you in relation to these matters but you did ask for some insights. I should think you have attended your share of starting up in business and accounting for tradesmen courses. So this is by no means the only guide to attending pseudo-vocational courses. It is, however, a guide, and as such useful[1]. I don't want to labour this area of logistics. Much of this is common knowledge – or if not - it should be. I have written this in a fairly brusque style and I implicitly seek your permission to do so[2]. Apologies if it offends. If you are prepared to just wing it, then disregard the rest of this letter. If you are happy to read on, then I would emphasise that once you choose the programme for you, then as all good courses go, the key to success and enjoyment is being prepared.

Some courses are run on a very militaristic basis where time and timings are integral to the delivery of the programme. Deviations are not tolerated and group discussion or answering questions is kept under strict control lest the timetable be upset. Some courses are a veritable romp through the content and theory and a big free form

---

1 This is an often used expression on self-help programmes – it means that what follows is shite but someone wrote a book about it so don't dismiss it entirely.
2 Rob, I want you to take particular notice of the way I am writing – this extra deferential tone will become second nature on some courses. We become very good at asking permission to say things and, thus, honouring one another.

love-in cum treasure hunt, where anything can happen because the key to the success of the programme is not the delivery of knowledge, but the exchange of numbers and other personal data.

Whatever the style, forewarned is forearmed. For example, one cannot be buying plasters for one's blistered heels in the only Boots open this side of Holborn, while the trainer is starting the afternoon's teaching and allocating roles in the crucial role play. The show will go on without you and the learning opportunity will be lost. Perhaps even more importantly, new and crucial connections may be made during that activity and coming in late may mean you are stuck with the front row social worker guy from Norfolk who doesn't know why he came on the course, or the mid-life crisis disaffected "allied health professional" who wants to talk about her last boyfriend ad nauseum. Then again, depending on who you are in Boots with at the time you may be comfortable with that. Equally, one cannot travel from outside London – say, Europe or beyond – and pack for the weekend without bringing a change of undies or a second shirt. It's these little details that can make or break the social and networking elements of the course. So it's always best to know what one is in for and to that end one should ask up front at the time of booking – just as one would if booking a rental car or a hotel room – is this a non-smoking programme, will there be a lunch break, will one be allowed to ask questions, is there a dress code (e.g. striped sweatshirts mandatory, sneakers expected, yes or no to twinsets etc), how many drinks each night is too many and so on. Even the well-seasoned course attendee can forget to put on deodorant, especially if rushing out the door with the kids crying that Daddy makes them brush their teeth before eating, the toast burning, the phone ringing and the travel card lost under three nappies, a wodge of oily tissues and the scribbled on map of the course venue's location.

Despite the best of intentions, even the most process oriented punter can forget to pack a biro or lose one's notes at the cinema on the way home. Knowing ahead of time that replacement notes come at a price is always useful.

I am emphasising all of these matters because not only will a little forethought help you to enjoy the time you spend with these people (some of whom may be instrumental in referring clients to you in a few months), but also as any good student knows, the better impression you can make with the course coordinator the better your chance of passing and getting the hard earned certificate (or maybe being asked to come back as a tutor or facilitator next time around) despite absence, caustic remarks to the class dummy and generally misbehaving at the break up dinner.

So Rob, come prepared to say something of interest about yourself in the opening session. One can try to hang back in the pre-course registration and coffee, lurking in the corridor or toilet, or simply arriving late and filling the last seat. However, once the introductions are made by the facilitators this is one group activity you just can't opt out of.

Turning to what to say. Remember there are 30-60 nervous and startled middle age life coach wannabes poised ready to judge you. The good old "I am an I.T./HR/change management agent just looking for a bit more" starts to get a little old after the third one. In this regard there is no safety in numbers. Try to spice it up if you can because there is a good chance that your opening gambit will: a) be all they remember; b) make no difference to most of them but at least help you feel part of the crowd; or c) positively influence some of the group to want to work with you. At the very least it might entice someone to ask you to join them for lunch – better than kidding you are meeting a friend – no one still does that after they leave school. In your case though, your background may be both a feather in your cap as well as a turn off. Try to find a way to sell it to everyone. The last thing you want is some fellow participant offering you a blocked toilet and a cold beer at the end of the first day. I always find that an earthy Aussie blend of laconic humour, mixed with self effacing confidence works – or at least no one has said otherwise.

The other key time for having one's wits about one is in choosing where to sit in the room once the introductions are over and the teaching begins. Leave the front row for the aged, the swots and the nerds. It's not so much that you want to be at the back, as somewhere in the middle. Most importantly, the people you sit near will be the first people you connect with, so choose wisely. Also human beings are creatures of habit and you may find that the chair you take now is yours for the next 20 days, so again, think it through. When the chairs are filling up is not the time. Be strategic and if you know who you don't want to sit near already – this is after the introductions have been made so you really should have some idea – be proactive now. It's just like a classroom. You can still pass notes, roll your eyes and generally chivvy each other along as we did in Elizabethan Literature, but the going will be tough if you are trying to impress some small guy from Padstow who can't make eye contact and has predetermined that you are a high achieving smart arse from down under, or rather, in your case, a playboy plumber stumbled into the wrong room.

It can be a minefield. Things as simple as how to queue for the toilet can actually make or break those first impressions that we strived so hard to make positively and unthreateningly only 2 hours before. This can be a confronting time in the opening days as one works out whether one believes in jumping the queue by using the disabled facilities, whether one likes fresh air or stale in the plenary session room, whether one likes to speak first or last in the break out group work sessions, indeed whether one likes to let anyone else speak in the breakout sessions.

There are no doubt a myriad of other issues for men as well. I gather that a lot of posing and grandstanding can go on. I'm not au fait with the men's urinals etiquette and whether to talk or not, wash hands or not etc. Not that these rules should be any different on courses. However, I can even rely on my own observations to say, that the type of men on courses generally is not representative of the male population at large. I think that if you still retain some of the good looks and charm which you had in abundance when we met at university, then you will be quite a novelty on a self-help style programme. Having said that, it doesn't follow that you will instantly find yourself more relaxed or at ease. Even you may be thrown when breaking into a conversation over tea the first morning, innocently believing everyone is a stranger, when you find the other two people are in fact husband and wife and in the throes of a subdued, yet highly personal and embarrassing domestic altercation. It's often not the doing but the extricating that sorts the wheat from the chaff, as it were.

Should one talk to the trainers or facilitator team in the coffee break? What does it say about you if you are the only one to do so? How many sweets are too many? What sort of ring tone should you have? The list goes on.

I find as a general rule that less is more on the first weekend. No one really cares who you are and everyone is likely to hate you anyway, because you are never going to be that person they all love right off the mark. She is generally much more giggly, pretty, younger, perter and less intimidating than you on your mildest day. So don't even bother trying. As I was told towards the end of my course, you are pegged right from the start and a lot will come down to your competitive nature and whether there is a more A type man (or woman) in the room. I would suggest that you just use the breaks wisely and make a beeline for someone who said something you found genuinely interesting in the opening remarks. If no such person exists or you can't get near them, then be sure to have the Blackberry handy for a few urgent emails that need attending to. Better to be the loser workaholic who can't switch it off, than the loser.

Just like at university where the person who laughed at something I said in the first tutorial (you, as it happened) was likely to be my friend for the year, the same applies on courses. Though it may depend on what the amusing remark was – so just temper your usual wit in the interests of appearing seemly. Also, recognise that lots of people don't have an actual sense of humour and are hard of hearing, so don't get carried away by overall merriment when you speak – it may simply be that everyone is being polite or God forbid, laughing at the private joke at your expense they all shared over lunch. Maybe just have a couple of brief yet witty anecdotes up your sleeve to help break the ice and even convey a certain joie de vivre (something sadly lacking in the realm of self help programmes – it has to be said). It's all about moderation though. Don't be that guy who never shuts up and thinks he is the funniest person in the room.

A very important topic for the start of the course is what to wear, especially, footwear. While there is something to be said for the comfortable all purpose sneakers, just make sure they are in keeping with the rest of the ensemble. I know that you now favour a heavier work boot and pushed down sock combination. You would certainly pull that off with ease and panache while laying hosepipes in suburban Brisbane. However, they are casual and the line between cool and frumpy is a fine and hard to pinpoint thing. I think that shorts and boots are not really de rigeur anymore (i.e. for people knocking on 40). I would say that the shoe says more than you think about yourself. Do you want all that attention and the raised eyebrows? Maybe try something in a colour. I find that as long as it is not a grey slip-on loafer circa 1983 or a Velcro fastening white shoe, then you probably can't go too far wrong. And clean is great.

Now while you will think this does not pertain to you, I do have to say something about make-up. Not that you will be wearing any. But a few tips to guide you may come in handy. Beware, as you might in normal human concourse, of too much. Being a self help programme one needs to bear in mind one's views about tears and emotions. This is such a big area that my course actually had a whole weekend dedicated to it as a coaching issue and something for coaches to be aware of in themselves. In this regard they might have spent a little more time on the problems occasioned by an excess or a dearth, rather than on merely naming the various emotions.

In relation to cosmetics and intimate personal presentation I should say this: don't go without completely. Unless you have Christy Turlington looks or George Clooney's presence we all need a little concealer, or a touch of lip gloss (or balm and breath freshener). A hair brush through the old locks at some stage in the preceding week is not a bad idea. Accept that lipstick will streak and run with all the talking and nail biting that will ensue – so don't be too critical. Watch out for the tears. I would recommend that women wear mascara advisedly. Whatever you do, there are risks. If you cry and it runs you look like a racoon and lose credibility. If you cry and it doesn't, you look too good to be true and too well prepared for the tears to be genuine. Bear that in mind Rob, as you will witness tears at some point.

Women are going to talk about clothes and make-up; it is a way of bonding between the girlier girls. Don't be tempted to join in though. A wry smile from a benign distance will be better than an involved analysis of the season's hues. I would recommend that you don't comment on looks at any time other than to admire, and then not lecherously or lasciviously. The course letch is despised and hated beyond the walls of the course venue. He/she always waits until the break up drinks or dinner to show his/her true colours, but we all know who it is long before that. If you do talk cosmetics and fashion they will assume you are gay (yes, even you).

Oh yes - bring some deodorant. Carry a bag large enough and masculine enough to conceal it though. No man-bags. The stress of revealing your innermost secrets can occasion some perspiration. Also the weather can be changeable and the lunch time journey outside of the room can often be exerting. A clean hanky? Fresh socks daily? Some sort of colour coordination? Not too many zippers, pockets or earth tones. You might want to come with a signature style in mind. The all black or all charcoal look is fetching and adds some intrigue, providing nothing shines.

Maybe I insult you. I don't mean to suggest that you are unable to dress or conduct yourself in this milieu.

It is just that I know from bitter experience that some men lose the plot on any sort of course or away-day. I sat next to my lawyer boss on a departmental away day wearing a sleeveless pale blue muscle shirt and tight beige board shorts. I can't remember a word he said but to this day (and it is 7 years ago now) I can still conjure an image of those pale, bulky biceps working their magic on the room as he drew up the complex diagram of the new transaction on the white board. I felt like a freak, a pervert. Where was I to look? Also the watering eyes and sneezing occasioned by the aftershave pulsing out of those very same pale pores...

At the other end of the spectrum, I was once asked by a colleague on a team building exercise involving building forts and finding buried treasure, to hold a sweaty, brown, polyester suit jacket. Seriously.

One final tip is that it is always appreciated when one is willing to contribute to discussions. One can't really embark on an experiential programme of discovery and not say anything for six months. Many try to. For the rest of the room, earnestly trying to learn and take notes, it is a toss-up between the compulsive contributor with an uncanny grasp of the obvious and the strong silent chin in hand type by the back door, as to who is more infuriating. Try to engage at even a superficial level with fellow participants in the social settings the course offers. Oh and harden oneself to feedback. It comes in all sort of ways and often when you least expect it. I have to stress that in preparing one's opening gambit, thinking through one's outfits and devising conversational ploys, one must also be cognisant of the fact that how one responds in the moment can undermine all that preparation, damage all of those solid foundations and even render one unfit to continue the programme. We had a couple of drop-outs – work apparently intervened.

Now, it is stating the obvious, but don't lose it with the other participants, Rob. Better to bite your tongue and smile ruefully than engage in full-scale argument. And don't be the guy who is so repressed and uncomfortable about emotion that he winds up trampling on everyone who opens up any sort of discussion with or about feelings. There is a view that women "do" certain feelings well and naturally. One of my colleagues and I exchanged views when he expressed his discomfort with certain emotions displayed by women (or at least me). These emotions (I think it involved getting cross) were apparently unseemly for the weaker sex and purely the domain of men (cave men that is). If the purpose of the course is to teach you how to listen and raise awareness in your client, then keep the lid on opinions that stifle, judge or censor the clients you practise on.

Moving on to some of the content, you will be expected to learn some core skills like listening and questioning and being present and empathetic. So it's not rocket science but if done well, the power to raise awareness and transform lives and perspectives, is phenomenal. Done badly and you come off looking like a cross between an 10 year old running a mock TV interview and a *Goodies* skit. Just remember there isn't really a right or wrong with questions. As most of the people on my course were English there was very little risk of anyone asking too rude or too direct a question.

Nothing will be as difficult to answer in my view, as the dreaded "how did the baby come out?" or indeed "how did the baby get in there?" asked by your five year old son, in any case.

Another core skill is learning to be "in the moment". I think you have this one mastered. But act as if it is hard for you, as this will raise your currency with the more sensitive women, as you appear to master it so brilliantly over the duration of the course. It will raise the bar for the male attendees who will be driven to compete with you. As a result, the quality will improve. Not to mention the "norming, forming and storming" of the group dynamic.

I am conscious that I have gone on at some length so I should start to wrap this letter up. I want to just make a final point – all courses have their own culture and jargon and lingo. If you pick it up quickly you will be not only credible and seem clever, but you will also be able to throw it in conversations with the HR professionals in the room. This could help you if you want to be retained for their in-house coaching needs.

Here are a few to master straight off:

"My stuff" - this should not to be confused with "your stuff" or just plain old "stuff".

"Designing your ethos as a coach" – take your time, you need to evolve.

"Co-creating" – a coaching relationship primarily, but anything really.

"What will that look like?" – This pertains to outcomes and desires fulfilled, not so much people, new kitchens, cars or food.

"Did that land with you?" – a hugely overused expression. Be careful not to bring it too much into your real life.

"Honour" is a big deal – everyone should be honoured.

"Check-in" – this is something you learn to do with each other at specific times in order to see how things are going, not the coat check at reception.

"Endings" – do you do them? Some people don't apparently. Aspire to "dance in the moment".

Good luck.

Best wishes and I hope you find it as fulfilling and richly rewarding as I did.

T x

23 September, 2008

Dear Mum,

It was great to speak to you this morning. You sounded good in spite of the puréed food and the tiredness you described. Not much happening here. I had a very quiet day in the office today. No one spoke to me, which in itself is not bad. It lets one focus on the engrossing detail of being the "third pair of eyes" to check an extraordinarily interesting piece of subordinate legislation, to do with notification procedures in relation to promoters of tax mitigation schemes that are deemed notifiable. I was finding it a little heavy going, I must admit, when the third redraft popped into the electronic inbox with a half hearted apology. As a result, I was part way through reviewing a document that the drafting lawyer was still amending and changing, but I was not informed of what the changes and amendments were. If they had marked up the changes it would be some sort of help. However, like the dutiful civil servant that I am, I binned the second draft and started again on my 15 pages of double sided turgid law, looking for goodness knows what errors. My head was numb with the sheer effort of holding it up and my eyes were aching from poring over the minute font in the footnotes, that set out in laborious detail the chapter and verse of all the amending regulations that had preceded the new one I was reviewing.

I had a flashback during this of the time I spent drafting tax law in Canberra in the nineties and the great sense of accomplishment I had when my words found their way into the statute books. Fancy feeling satisfaction and accomplishment at the new and fresh, easy to read style of the legislation that was setting a higher and more exacting standard for generations to come. I was so young then, so ambitious and idealistic.

If you are having trouble getting to sleep I think I have just the thing...

I know you're thinking: "Yes, but love, all jobs have their tedious aspects. Just be grateful you can leave mid-afternoon to pick up the children from school." I know that is true. I know that standing on the checkouts at K-mart was also a trial. And actually for tedium, the life guard at the gym pool probably has the plum job.

Every two hours he fills a little tube with pool water and shakes it and writes something down (probably a urine analysis) and then he wanders around the pool and picks up the odd float left out – usually mine that I am still using - and then he sits down and watches the three or four swimmers swim. Then he has a busy period from 4 to 6pm when about 25 kids jump and splash and scream in a space the size of your hospital room. Goodness knows what he thinks about for the other 10 hours of the day that he spends in that subterranean chlorine reeking grotto.

The other day it was just me doing my self-styled aqua-aerobic routine at the far end of the pool, while he tried to look anywhere but at me, when two official and head officey looking fellows appeared and started talking to him with their clipboards. I am sure they were trying to work out ways of maximising the capacity and profit making attributes of the pool, given it is pretty empty 4-5 hours of the gym day. Maybe they will find a way to drain it and use it for kiddies' football or ballet which are ever so popular, and for which they could extract an additional fee from all the anxious, desperate mothers and carers at their wits end in winter to amuse their poppets. It's amazing what you get for your gym pound. We have frequent plumbing problems (Rob could certainly clean up here with the ancient pipes, central heating and often non-English

speaking workforce to compete with); ranging from the leaking tap
at the by-the-pool-shower head, to three out of six ladies locker
room showers being out of order. Other problems have included:

Shower head fallen off;

Ceiling plaster fallen down;

Flooding of stalls due to blocked drains;

Tiles loose from walls;

Banging pipes;

Blocked and unusable toilets;

Broken lifts;

Locker door dangling precariously by one screw;

Toxic cleaning products of industrial abattoir strength so as to
cause bleeding eyes (well, it felt that bad).

Given that the locker room is located somewhere near or under
the Picadilly line, it is not a little concerning that so much is going
wrong. Perhaps that thought has only occurred to *me*. What is
baffling is how a drain built to serve three showers gets blocked. It's
not as though we are all washing our dirty dishes in there, or
throwing our chewing gum and burger wrappers down them. The
storm water drains in the streets can cope with assorted debris, dirt,
effluent even, and yet purpose built shower drains can't cope with a
little water, soap scum and, I daresay, hair. Maybe it's a question of
maintenance or perhaps it's all for show. If they block access to the
facilities often enough e.g. broken lifts to the pool and main gym,
unusable ladies toilet, no service to internet accessible computers, not
to mention contaminated pool itself ("chemical imbalance"– god
forbid what are we swimming in?!) then they can justify increasing
the monthly membership fees on the basis that one does not want
to continue to get what one has paid for.

It's all part of the "rip off Britain" mentality that nothing good
could ever be cheap. If I dwell on this too long I will become very
despondent. Is it that hard to run a gym and make a little profit? I

know real estate and staff and milk and petrol and heating and cooling costs and all the other inputs to running a gym are high in central London, not to mention the Power Plates vibrating machines that exercises your atrophied butt muscles while you sit or stand on them, that must cost a bomb to buy (and of course the cost of reinforcing the floors to boot), but £1.90 for a tea bag in hot water?

And what have they done with the members' noticeboard? There used to be a sense of community and camaraderie around the notice board. French lessons, babysitting/ironing, flat to rent, maybe even Personal Coaching. It used to seem that we, the members, were not alone but joined in harmony striving for a better shape, a more toned thigh, a flatter stomach and a trimmer and healthier lifestyle. It felt that the personal trainers walked the floor looking for ways to offer helpful suggestions on how to pulse it out to tighten those abs, or even some gait analysis for free. But now, the whole corporate image and branding thing has been taken up a notch. As a result, what must be head office initiatives seem to have depersonalised some aspects of the membership. Even so, I do applaud the staff for their commitment and dedication. Turnover seems low, smiles are broad and genuine. Faced with frequent plumbing issues and complaining members, they remain calm and good humoured. In spite of all the above, the Gym remains a haven for me. A respite on the way to or from work. A safe and enabling environment for the children during those seemingly endless weekends in winter when Andrew is away and the need to get them out of the house is like a primal urge. Where would I be without the Gym?

Are you managing the three walks each day around the floor? How are the meals?

I should let you go and take a walk. I will retire. I need to check that Tommy is still under his covers. The other night he called out: "Too dark Mummy. Put the light on Mummy". It was 3:15 in the morning so I stumbled down to shush him and check what the problem was only to find no sign of him in his bed (mattress on floor). I could hear him telling me to make it light but I could not see or feel him. In fact all I could see was Felix who was actually on Tommy's mattress, seemingly having rolled over, so I feared poor old Tommy was stuck under Felix. But as my addled brain defuzzed and the sleepy veil of fog drifted from across my half shut eyes, something made me reach under Jack's bed, and there he was; lost in the dark and the dust, unable to find his way out to fresh air and space. By this stage, in giggles, we decided he should come and sleep in my bed. He thereupon helped himself to big finger full of Vicks Vapour Rub and went back to sleep with his knees in my back. Having a Daddy who works abroad has its compensations.

Much love

Tx

26 September, 2008

Dear Mum,

Glad Rob got my note. Sorry to hear he has decided not to become a coach for now. I suppose all the recent rain makes his current business more viable. I hope the mouth ulcers are not too painful. How is Dad managing? He must be so tired; but cooking so much offal? One of the few upsides to having one's spouse in hospital.

I am sure you are right when you say coaching can be for everyone. Think of all the people who struggled with life's hurdles right down through history. Nothing a little bit of deep listening and awareness raising questions and action planning could not have fixed.

Think of Lizzie Bennet, or better still, Jane and that drippy Bingley, Atticus Finch, Miss Faversham, poor old abandoned Paddington Bear. Not to mention George Doubleya. Coaching might have been transformational for them. Mind you, one of the philosophical underpinnings of coaching is that the client is creative, resourceful and whole. So maybe not everyone is suitable as a client...

Jack came home from school early today with a rash – a virus called Slapped Cheek. He looks very red in the face – or "blushed" as he calls it. He is not unwell, merely uncomfortable. He is helping Andrew sweep up some leaves in the garden at the moment. Andrew has been back since Thursday – this is the fourth day - he seems to be enjoying a little London tranquillity after the pace and mayhem of Lagos. We spent Saturday in the Cotswolds and yesterday with friends in Richmond. Then yesterday evening we all worked in the garden for a while. It was a late summer frenzy of clearing and pruning. I hope the rash is in fact Slapped Cheek and not some weird reaction to the plants or poisonous chemical bug spray Andrew detoxifies the shrubs with...

I have decided that the damp lawn that is unusable and actually overrun by ivy could well house an enclosed trampoline. I saw dozens of them in Brisbane in August. We might jump on that band wagon and keep up with the Ozzy Joneses. I figure it will amuse the boys and me all through the winter. I might have some decking put in around it so that it becomes a feature, like an arbour or a fountain. Maybe I can train the ivy, which currently sucks the life out of the soil and prevents grass from growing, to move up and over the netting around the trampoline and create a private little bouncy haven...

Meanwhile, we have to consider a move. The three boys love sharing their bedroom but even so when all the beds and mattresses are out and occupied there are 2 square feet of floor space left. Ceajf[J G

lchaw[yf   n[8yva

Sorry, I had to get my bearings there. Andrew has made dinner – his once every 4 months beef curry extraordinaire - and my eyes are stinging and watering form the garlic fumes. A sensation not unlike that in the pool areas after a hazmat cleaning crew has done the pool surrounds at the gym. One of Jack's spelling words is "fume". I must remember to provide the definition tomorrow based on this rather painful experience. I might need to take some of Jack's antihistamine. Not to whinge about having a meal cooked for me. Long may that continue. But there is a tendency among men who do cook to really overegg the pudding. Remember when Dan was making baked fish when we were in Brisbane? The amount of time and effort that went into the optional breadcrumb stuffing alone was something to see. You and Dad were so engrossed in the rugby that you missed the micromanaging and delegation going on in the kitchen. I ate three bowls of the children's spaghetti Bolognese while those pine nuts roasted. Andrew is the same. He spends so long dicing and chopping and noisily slurping his oil based sauces (thank goodness I persuaded him to change from palm nut oil and butter, to olive, all those years ago or I would be obese, diabetic and fighting heart disease by now) that by the time the meal is served I am either full of other munchies because I grew tired of waiting, or so tired and past eating, that I offend with my lack of interest.

Anyway, I was thinking we could get the boys enthusiastic about a triple bunk bed – like on a submarine – so as to delay moving for a while. If we can hold out long enough and streamline the hoarding and saving of every bit of paper that comes through the door (this is the children in particular who want to cherish all the kiddies colouring sheets from family restaurants), then we won't have to rush to buy a bigger flat just yet. This restaurant paper policy is not exactly environmentally friendly. On the one hand we indoctrinate them about recycling and reusing and then grab multiple packs of crayons and blank paper every time we step out for a meal in a restaurant, a visit to a child free zone, or Sunday mass, and bring back several copies of what they give out in-house as well (restaurants and church, that is). I suppose we could rely on etch-a-sketches but the novelty would wear off quickly.

Maybe restaurants could invest in mini-electronic whiteboards. Not just every classroom, but every café and indeed, every home, should have one. Then the little punters could email their drawings to their email accounts and load them up onto their MySpace area. The mind boggles. Some parents recommend Gameboys and Playstations but that is a slippery slope.

Anyway, I am sure we can come up with uses for all those drawings and pictures currently filling up bags and boxes in cupboards around the house. Perhaps I could get an awning for the trampoline and then hang some of the artwork around the walls of the ivy clad netting fence thing. Maybe we can keep them for added insulation in the ceiling of our bedroom where the layer between us and the guy upstairs is like a well worn wafer and we can hear every breath he takes. It's not that I have a problem throwing things away – quite the contrary - but I do think they will enjoy rediscovering their art work in later life.

I know that when I see those Mother's day cards and the macaroni necklaces I made for you when I was little, it really thrills me. A bit like rereading essays I wrote in history at uni or perusing old maths books full of calculus. I am amazed I ever knew all that stuff. Remember when you used to hear me studying and ask questions so I could prepare for exams. All that turgid detail in land law? Things don't change though, do they? Here you are *reading* all the turgid detail, only somewhat less cohesive and well organised. We did have fun though in Year 8 English making up songs about the size of Mrs Copperfield's rear. And all those school plays – it was great that you kept those smocks from the 60s. That high necked calico mini dress must have seen me through the *Importance of Being Ernest, Romeo and Juliet, Grapes of Wrath* and even a last supper or two. Does one capitalise the Last Supper? Or italicise? Or just put into inverted commas? I imagine that if Slapped Cheek gets capitals then...

I will sign off now and go and enjoy some beef and rice with my garlic.

Much love

Tx

27 September, 2008

Dear Mum,

Dad tells me the chest pains were probably oesophageal ulcers and can be treated. Poor you. Dad sounded well. He was trying to be very upbeat and reassuring, as always. Dad also said your spirits are very good despite all the discomfort and side effects. I wish I was there, very much.

I spent another brilliant day in the office. I was again checking some statutory instruments to be laid before Parliament next month. I was overcome with a sense of great isolation. I had an out of body experience where I saw myself at that desk, making no difference nor altering the course of human endeavour, history or pretty much anything at all. It's not that I shuffle paper around immersed in issues and imponderable problems that need years of scrutiny and analysis. No, rather, it's that we work to real deadlines creating impenetrable rules that are truly meaningless. They are not only poorly expressed; they actually cease to have any real impact.

Somewhere in the Chancellors Budget address he says: "We will fight tax avoidance and revenue leakage", and we all cheer. Eight months later I am reduced to a caffeine guzzling wreck, wondering what the hell I am doing with my life. Maybe I take it too personally. After all it is not as if the Government is setting out to destroy my self esteem. Is it? Rather, each new enactment or policy pronouncement actually creates half a dozen new jobs or new temporary assignments. I should feel honoured to have such an important role in maintaining the Exchequer and helping the cogs turn smoothly and efficiently.

Perhaps I am just feeling morose due to a sense of dislocation and frustration at my powerlessness to help you. I should have studied medicine as you suggested in 1987. You can now say "I told you so".

Some days at work are better than others. Last week I went to a team meeting which held a lot of promise as we, four of us, were all joined in a comradely saunter through the many corridors of the building in search of the designated meeting room. We passed people who had Digestives and bakewell tarts on the shared shelves, we saw beautiful and varied art work and we got to hear Big Ben chiming from various sets of open windows. At our meeting we discussed some of the members of the office and their various moves and promotions, the philosophical underpinnings of our team's work and its recent challenges. Finally, I made a contribution, when I suggested we discuss the content of the new department learning and development plan, much to the amusement of my colleagues who were able to:

a)   claim they had not brought it (this is a euphemism for not read nor ever intend to read it);

b)   refer to its many typographical errors; and

c)   comment on the misnaming of our department within the document – thereby clearly proving that they had read it, and that it is in fact a plan borrowed or copied from another department.

Nothing like feeling part of an organisation that cares.

This actually proved to be a very fruitful conversation. I learnt a lot about the wider civil service attitude to training lawyers. We managed to extract a further 10 minutes discussion, deferred proper consideration of the learning plan to a later date and left feeling very jolly indeed.

Anyway enough of this. I intended to write with some interesting news. Shall I tell you a little about recent events at school? Always a sure fire pick-me-up!

The new term has started well. The boys seem to have settled in with their new teachers happily. We had an infants' assembly on Wednesday. It's theme was talents. Don't hide your light under a bushel; use the gifts God gave you. All the children had to say what their special gift is. I must say that the football and art worlds are in for a huge influx of ability in about 15 years from now. Funny how the gifts that really are the hardest to develop and market are the ones the children believe they have in abundance. Where are the kids saying – sense of humour, spelling, helping my mum? Heck even just "I am good at riding my bike and eating sweets" would ring true for a 6 year old.

Having said that, I guess the current generation of under 10s is more driven and scheduled than we ever were. I remember pestering you until I was blue in the face to do ballet like Claire and every time you said "next year", knowing I would outgrow the interest. No doubt also knowing it would not be one of my gifts. All those fat little girls in their tutus and slippers feeling so princessy and demure...

And I wound up with three sons...

Speaking of children's activities, I had occasion to wonder again whether I am raising backward neophytes, heralding from the 1970s rather than the 2000's. I overheard some mothers at the gym last week discussing their children's schedules. I mean, who under 25, who is not at least a management consultant, even has a schedule. These children have judo and swimming, French and art, ballet and chess, Spanish and music and cycling proficiency, drama and gymnastics. One of Jack's classmates has such a full week on school days that he has to do his Italian, pilates, rugby, mandarin and science on the weekend, between mass, swimming, lunch and 23.5 minutes free play. Something will have to give when the homework really starts and the first communion classes kick in – not to mention the boy scouts, altar serving and volunteerism.

I was really fascinated by the cycle proficiency class. I think I borrowed a bike from a kid up the road and rode around the cul-de-sac over two Sundays and became proficient that way in those heady, sepia days in the seventies. I was 8 and clearly under achieving since I was not at Cantonese or Pottery at the time, but actually had Sundays available...

Having said all of that I am not scoffing at the desire to enrich and broaden and expose one's offspring. Goodness, no. There are clearly a few holes in the market though, which is where I need to step in. Just imagine if we could enhance the skills in negotiation, face-to-face communications, street smarts, rapping, tidying up, pocket money budgeting and for the younger ones, bottom wiping. There is no doubt demand for maximising the effectiveness of the tantrum - a session on style, another on timing and another where we really hone in on more sophisticated manipulation.

Maybe I could offer sibling packages and cover all the age groups as well as the nitty gritty of sibling rivalry. I could really make a difference in the holiday camp market place.

And for the mums? And dads! Well I need to be pretty strategic about catching the interest in that discerning sector, but couples classes could work, or coffee mornings with a twist, where we workshop some issues of concern. Maybe a series of classes, free latte included in the fees. Topics could include:

How to say "no" and mean it.

I know my child is average and that's ok.

How to dress your child for their body shape.

Restaurant voices.

Boundaries are cool.

Play doesn't have to be hard work.

I could have fridge magnets made with little thoughts printed on them, so that whenever the parents glance at the activities schedule for the term or the good behaviour star chart upon which they would magnetically reside, they would be reminded of something useful, such as "if it walks and talks like a child, it must be a child".

Did I ever tell you about the star chart that our then nanny, Helga, made when I went back to work last year? She was struggling to get the boys to do as she wanted so we decided the chart might incentivise better behaviour. It really needed to go in a spreadsheet – there was so much detail. There were at least 10 categories for each child, based on their age (then just 2, 4 and 6) and abilities. And it was a bugger to administer. For example, if Felix walked home from nursery, rather than rode on the buggy board, he got a star. If Tommy ate with a spoon rather than fingers, he got a star. If Jack said please and thank you, he got a star. Half the hoped for actions were already mastered and long since acquired habits; the other half were not desirable from any one's point of view; for example, chopping with Mummy's scissors.

Did I tell you about the time she took me aside to say that she was very concerned about Jack's maths skills? He was apparently unable – at age 5 - to do subtraction sums such as 15 takeaway 23 or 9 minus 17. I had to explain that the negative integers were possibly a little beyond the year ones just yet, maybe in second term. Fearful that we in the UK were backward and all of the ex-soviet Eastern European children are racing ahead (explains things like arms wars, if they can master the old trigonometry and trajectories early), I did explain to Jack that there are numbers less than zero and that they are useful for measuring things like temperatures. Also handy if you go under the sea and you want to work out your depth in relation to the surface of the water. He was able to then extrapolate the concept and suggest – "or like if someone is really naughty, they get a negative star on the chart".

Maybe Helga is on to something after all.

The learning for me is that the real world context really aids with knowledge retention and learning. To that end, I was telling the boys about the time when I was about 9 and the strip of purple flowered wall paper was ripped off the toilet wall and you had to employ strong arm tactics to break us down and force a confession out of us; culminating in James confessing in order to get our TV privileges restored. This was by way of explaining the meaning of "criminal investigation".

Anyway, the star chart was a little unwieldy. There were so many stars on that chart by the end of the first day that I started to fear that local stationery shops would be unable to keep up with demand. While well-intended, the chart was not capable of operating as an incentivisation programme at all. Maybe in communist regimes star charts operated differently. Certainly, the purpose behind Helga's was never clear. It did excite them as they begged for more and more multicoloured stars though, every evening. I still find one or two in the washing machine every now and then. And I think Helga probably enjoyed ruling all the lines and writing in all the boxes and sitting as judge and jury all afternoon. Star charts are generally baffling I find. Jack created one for himself this evening and gave himself several stars for playing nicely with his brothers. He is working towards a new toy plane. The year one class chart last spring may have confused him. Miss Finucane explained it well though – Jack had very few stars because he was a quiet student who was no trouble and got on with his work beautifully. It seems then that I have had it all wrong. Maybe I need one myself.

You will be tired out now reading all of this. I hope the photos find some sort of a home on your windowsill there – albeit a temporary one. Love to everyone else.

Xx

27 September, 2008

Dear Mum,

I am having a little chuckle to myself as Jack just wrote a note to himself, to remind him to tell Felix's best friend tomorrow to hate Felix. Felix just told him that was rude and walked away. The dramas of life at 4 and 6, eh?

I was at the gym today. I am always struck in the change room at the way the English and European women wander around naked and semi-naked, while down in Australia the women change in little cubicles or under and behind towels. It is remarkable how uninhibited they all are here. They love getting their "kit off", whether it is in the gym change rooms or on the beach. The whole idea that certain shapes really should not wear a bikini is completely foreign and unheard of in Europe. We in Australia, so laid back about so much, are pretty up tight by comparison. I would not dream of baring my stomach after three children, and yet by most standards, I am on the slimmer side of the fence.

You will be pleased to know that in honour of my birthday and the fact that women of a certain age look better with shorter hair cut into a style, I had my hair cut the other day. I told this beautiful Natalie Imbrugliaesque girl of about 24, that I wanted a whole new look and was keen on that of Keira Knightly at a recent film premiere: a short bob, tucked in close to the neck and just long enough to put behind the ears. Natalie looked very dubious and pretended to give this great consideration only to finally announce that given the shape of my face and the fact it is quite a long oval I would not suit such a short style but should consider a longer and more gentle look, where I retain the option to put my hair up or grow it just a little, to return to the more familiar territory of shoulder-length-no-layers-worn-up-everyday (i.e. current no-style style).

I think the mention of Keira was the problem. I am sure she was thinking: "You have got to be kidding. There is no way you can claim to look like her, you silly old frump. Let's just accept you are a sad old try-hard and give you a style that is consistent with your seniority and conservatism." And so she did just that, and proudly informed me that I looked both younger and more sophisticated after she was finished, throwing me into a slump in self esteem where I suddenly realised, I alone am deluded as to my true age and appearance.

Romping around in the gym, playing with the children and rolling in and out of work, is not keeping me young and fit, but aging me and wearing me out. A minimal alcohol intake of one glass of white wine per week, non smoking, non-drug taking, briskly walking about town, is not helping me. It is time to face reality. I have grey roots, teenage acne and distinguished smile lines at my eyes. In short, I look like an old crone with a hormone imbalance. Oh sure, I scrub up well enough and these things are always relative, but the truth is, none of us are oil paintings and certainly not what we once were. Haircut day was a day of massive realisation. It dawned on me in a whole new way why magazines with celebrities' cellulite and stars without make-up, sell.

But to what end? In the interests of the environment, animal welfare and feminism to boot I propose we all throw away the beauty mags and just get real. Sure, make some effort, but give away the extreme glamour and the Oscar night glitz for a little bit of realism. No one is a princess and all of this show and falsity helps no one. People will accuse me of being some sort of bra burning kill joy hippy, giving up on life. But the irony of it all is just shocking. Huge salaries and endorsement packages are awarded to peddle utter crap that serves no purpose other than promoting empty status symbols. It is medieval. Are we all so gullible and childlike that we believe that buying that perfume will ensure we too will make records, look glamorous and secure a cool, inarticulate footballer boyfriend?

This charade and the manipulation of so many girls and women by the media and the fashion industry has always repelled me. But it was good to be reminded again of just how powerful all of that can be if you fall into the trap of believing it matters. Luckily, now, I can say that within 36 hours of that haircut my malaise over my lack of sophistication and youth had disappeared. So some child thinks I am an old has-been. So, what if I am? All the better to launch my fragrance – "Tire". Anyway, I have my health, a means to earn a decent living, beautiful children and husband, home, hobbies and friends to boot. A few grey hairs, some smile lines? That is ok. The most important thing is that I can laugh and be grateful for what I have. Having said all of that, London Fashion Week brings in £20 million to the local economy, so I clearly have no idea what I am talking about.

You will be annoyed perhaps at such preoccupations - given your own state of brunch coat wearing, hair falling out, glamour. Mum, I am sure you look as good as anyone with leukaemia does. You could be a poster girl for cancer care or leukaemia support.

How is Dad? I have been trying to call him but I seem to miss his times at home, given the time difference. Give him all my love and lots from Andrew and the boys as well, but keep a good amount for yourself too.

Txx

28 September, 2008

Dear Mum,

I pray that the nausea will have abated by the time you read this and that you are on some sort of road to recovery from those ulcers very soon. I have been trying to think of something to send that might cheer you up. Was the soap nice? We bought it at the gift shop at Kew Gardens last week.

The boys amused themselves browsing in the small but interesting children's section where they could press the stomach area on some stuffed birds and most life like sounds were emitted. Bird calls, that is. Ironically, while waiting for them to put the various birds back, a life like sound emanated from a nearby shopper as well. She was well into her 60s though, so we forgave her.

Tommy has, in that vein, been very expressive in his descriptions of everything of late. He told a packed post office last week that he had some wind. A few stifled giggles and startled looks did not deter him though, as he went on to tell me: "Don't worry Mummy. Everyone poos". Too true, you will be saying, given the disturbances you have suffered due to the chemo.

I have managed to secure another coaching client which brings my database of clients up to four. I am delighted to have met this new chap. He recently left a job in a bank and he is my first "big shot" client. We have begun discussing his options for the economic downturn, in particular, how he can use this time to regain some of his lost hobbies and interests. He is prepared to pay full fare for the sessions which is really encouraging. I met him through a former work mate, Sonia, at Shallack and Partners. She is now on maternity leave but he was a client of hers until quite recently. Sonia and I were reminiscing about the good old days when we were both at Shallack. It seems like a lifetime ago. She is having her first child in three weeks. She made partner and has been trying for a baby for several years so it is wonderful for her to be in the home straight now.

We first met in 1998 at Chargem and Weap LLP where we were newbies in the tax department. They flung us together since we were both Australian; there was a view that Aussies and Kiwis are fungible and hence should be seated together, trained together and generally made the butt of jokes en masse. Not sure what things are like in that sort of firm nowadays, but back then it was woeful. I remember all too well the struggle to work out an entirely new tax system and the detail of its laws without ever asking a question, leaving work before 9pm or being seen to be less than flat out busy. The duplicity and scheming was frightening, indeed, awe inspiring. I would say if you can make it there, you really could make it anywhere. I was never going to cut it though, since I used to go to the gym at lunch, hence absenting myself for 80 minutes, rather than 18. I also never worked out how to remotely send email timed to leave my outbox at 2:30am. Consequently, I was perceived as something of a dud. I think my complaint about the sexual innuendo and the constant chauvinism probably didn't help either. Afterall, women had only four uses, sex objects, mother figures, toiling minion or the subject of the joke. To waltz in (from Australia and the civil service) and be unprepared to play any of those roles, not be young or blond and not even try to pretend to be one of those things, meant my days were numbered.

Glass ceiling? 8 floors of solid concrete, marble and branded notebooks and pens stood between the best female associates and the executive suites. I remember one day one of the partners told me that I looked "particularly fetching" as he delegated some boring VAT query (I had on a grey jacket over a grey shirt that had a slight pewter thread through it). I naively thought things were improving. How wrong I was. At performance review time my pathetic lack of wherewithal was exposed. My seemingly conscientious questions for more and better instructions from a delegating partner amounted to evidence of my lack of commerciality and ignorance.

Still, a great learning experience and a real eye-opener. All credit to the lawyers who stay and make it big. I read an interview in *The Lawyer* (even more depressing than *The Ecologist*) the other day. Some partner somewhere was boasting about his sleepless nights doing deals. I suppose there is no greater mark of a man and his success than the number of nights he spends away from the home poncing in the office, or out with clients at lap dancing clubs smoking cigars and boasting about his wine cellar.

You see Mum, this is what I was referring to when I mentioned the tedium and the mediocrity and the striving. It's all frightfully banal and depressing. Somehow the annual trip to somewhere trendy is meant to compensate for all those hours in the office, knocking back machine coffee and bags of crisps, never seeing your family and criticising your subordinates, and more often than not resenting the treadmill, the other partners and the size of your waistline. The City and the system perpetuates the myth that a successful career in a firm that bears the moniker "magic" or "big" or "bulge bracket" is worth more than a job selling shoes, or gardening or as a fund raiser for the National Trust. Sure it pays better...

Ideal jobs? Now that's a good question.

Stone mason.

Chocolate tester.

Personal stylist to someone funny and interesting.

TV historian.

Writer.

Photographer.

Cross stitcher.

Mattress tester.

Or someone doing something really good and virtuous, making a difference. Say, fighting Aids, or poverty or prejudice, educating children, saving babies from disease... doctor, nurse, firefighter, sanitation worker.

Coach! Mother! Wife!

Night night Mum.

Tx

29 September, 2008

Dear Mum,

I am trying to decide whether to laugh or bang my head on something hard. Jack told me today that his teacher last year, commenting on one of his drawings which he took to school to share with her, said: "I don't think that looks like an Underground map. It just looks like a scribble to me." Given how expressive he is and how quick to report on the events of his day, I can only imagine he suppressed that memory til now. And why wouldn't he? I said that perhaps she was not looking carefully enough. He agreed and said: "Well she was *rather* boring and only likes girls". Goodness knows how she will be next year when Felix is in her class. I am not sure quite what he will do if someone criticises his art work. He told me today that I am "quite creative, but not really". I wonder where he gets his incredible self belief from. Oh, Daddy, perhaps? I will have to coach them and myself really well if the teacher is not in awe of his creations. I wonder if she would let me coach her? Mmm. The alternative might be to embrace the policy of candid and soul destroying feedback fot the under 8s and weigh in with some meaningful and timely constructive criticism for the children.

"No, Tommy, that is not a good wee in the toilet. You should have done it faster and sooner."

"Felix, why can't you colour in the lines? And those colours are all wrong - I have never seen a blue flower or a pink sun, you freak."

"Jack, you mis-spelt "mean" again, what is the matter with you?"

It must all seem very insignificant to you, Mum, but thanks for caring anyway.

Love

Tx

30 September, 2008

Dear Mum,

I gather the past couple of days have been pretty trying. You are in all our thoughts and prayers.

There is not much news here. I have been reflecting on all the times someone has given me advice and I have smiled demurely and quietly bitten my tongue. All the quips and rejoinders are never far from the tip thereof, but the belief that the other person is prepared to hear what I think is never as strong or well developed. Indeed more often than not when I have replied or stood up for myself or my point of view, I have found that the instinct that advocated silence was spot on. The silence, or glares or punishing distance that ensues is usually proof enough that keeping one's own counsel is the better path.

Now you are a woman who is forthright and wise. You speak your mind and seldom stand on ceremony. You have a rare blend of pragmatic positivity and magnetic good nature that lets you get away with that honesty. I fear I must lack some of that attractiveness of personality, for when I copy your style of candour, I usually come unstuck. Let me stress that I am not talking about being rude or flippant. Merely taking someone seriously and standing my ground in an honest and intelligent, respectful and dignified way, a remark in response seldom seems to work for me.

However, I am not so overcome with concern about the person who I want to respond to that I am always incapable of an honest reply. Rather, I feel that if they cannot take some of their own medicine then our relationship is not much to begin with. On the one hand that seems harsh and uncharitable; yet to not speak is to patronise the other person and assume they are less able to cope with a difference of opinion than I am. It becomes somewhat circular or even spiral. Have I perhaps over-analysed it? So this missive is going to vent those frustrations once and for all. I will try to cleanse myself of long held resentments and thereby purify my thinking and restore the equilibrium one feels when one is true to oneself.

Here goes:

What was said	*What I said/did*	*What I should have said*
Felix really should be in a nursery so he can learn to socialise.	Well I enjoy being at home with him. They grow up so fast.	Does he look poorly socialised? Clearly you were put into a nursery at a very tender age to learn these fabulous social skills.
Why do you park your baby's pushchair by the road?	It is hard to avoid doing that in central London.	Why do you care? What business is it of yours? The pavement is by the road by definition.
You risk your son taking up smoking if you tell him that it is bad for him.	Well I am only giving him the facts – there is a risk whether I say so or not.	You feel pretty bad that you smoke around your kids, eh?
Do you plan to breastfeed?	I will see how it all goes.	What business is that of yours you dirty old pervert? I will have you up for sexual harassment, asking me that in this elevator at work with 12 men in earshot.

Have you gained weight?	I don't know – do I look like I have?	Yes. Isn't it great?
Poor you – three boys.	Oh they are lovely and I think everyone loves what they get.	You rude old cow.
You look like a zombie.	I am a little tired.	So do you – but you don't have a waking baby at home do you?
You have not looked good for years.	Haven't I?	Wow. Thanks. Shall we do you now?

I feel so much better! I am noticing a pattern in the comments above. Maybe I need to think a little more about my appearance, or getting a thicker skin. Oops better go. Child crying out and it's almost 11pm. Hope it is not going to take a long time to settle him, as I look like a zombie.

Tx

29 September, 2008

Dear Mum,

I was very sad and concerned to hear how ill you felt today and how difficult you were finding it to breathe. I spoke with Claire when she got home from the hospital and she gave me a description of your symptoms and what the doctors were saying. Unfortunately, things progressed somewhat after that and a couple of texts from Dan apprised me that I should call Claire again. I gather Dad may stay with you through the night and that the suspected pleuritic infection might in fact be a collapsed lung. Glory be and Gordon Bennett! What next.

I am thinking of you all the time and praying and hoping for a speedy recovery from all these complications and that you will have the strength and resolve to fight on through these awful days. I love you Mummy. You are never out of my thoughts. I miss you.

Tx

29 September, 2008

Dear Claire,

Thanks ever so much for your call today and filling me in on events with Mum and the past day or two. As I said on the phone, I really feel for you all. It must be terrible to see her so uncomfortable and in pain and anguish. And to see Dad holding it together when he must feel so powerless and desperate, seems too much to bear. I don't really know how to help or be a support. From this distance I can merely listen and offer platitudes. I cannot imagine how it is in fact to be in the room while she is struggling to breathe, uncertain whether to sit or lie, to call for help or soldier on, and so on, as you described. It is terrible, terrible.

I know that I am probably in some sort of huge denial – or at least - I have been. Checking statutory instrument drafts for errors is only so engrossing, actually, so I can't say that my working life is helping take my mind off Mum. The children and my coaching is helping a lot to distract me – all of which gives me very much a sense of positivity and a conviction that all will be well and indeed that life goes on – cold as that would sound. I can see why you relish getting back to work with the homeless of north Brisbane! All of which only indicates the depth of our denial.

I feel incredibly helpless. I would love to jump on a plane right now and be with you. Truth is, I am not sure how I will even get there, if I do need to come. I am not sure what the prognosis will be for Mum, so it is hard not to think about alternate solutions. Does one bring one's children to these sorts of things? Dragging them out of school and across the world so that their Mummy can be near her very ill mother. Is it just unreasonable and likely to only cause Mum more stress and heartache? Will it impede her recovery. It is all so uncertain.

Maybe it is all moot and she will be ok.

I know that we cannot answer any of these questions now.

Please know you and all the family are constantly in my thoughts and that we all send our love and are praying furiously for a good result, soon.

Be brave Clairey. You are a rock. Know that I love you and miss you and cherish you.

Xx

30 September, 2008

Dear Mum,

I hope that the infection is under control. I heard from Claire and Dad just how much pain and difficulty you were in yesterday and I trust that the strong anti-biotics and the pain relief helped you somewhat through the night. Certainly an education in disease, drugs and treatments, this leukaemia thing, eh? So pneumonia, collapsed lung (pneumothorax) and a fungal infection in the other lung. You poor old thing. Praying that your system starts to recover from the chemo and you fight off all these infections very quickly.

All my love

Tx

PART TWO
The Middle...

2 October, 2008

Dear Mum,

As you are on the road to recovery now and starting to respond well to the cocktail of drugs, I wanted to share with you a little of the fun I have been having with my after school club at the boys' school. I have a group of ten children aged 9-11 with whom I am working to develop oral communications skills. So far we have discovered a lot of talent and quite a bit of confidence with speaking and role playing. We are learning a thing or two about listening and concentration skills as well. A few mothers of younger children have enquired whether I could run the class for those age groups next term. I would be delighted to do so.

As you know I really hope to build this up into a fully fledged business of children's communication coaching – both group and one-to-one, so the more experience and practice I can get, the better. I hope, in time, to work with children and young people for whom confident and articulate oral communication is not just a matter of improving on an already competent base, but for whom there is a risk that these skills will never otherwise be fostered. I don't just mean children in abusive or destructive situations (someone on my coaching course said – "so you can work with bullied kids to help them find their voice") but the many for whom interfacing with a computer or a phone is more interesting and easier than face to face contact. I am learning that the value of so-called communication coaching transcends the content and the articulated purpose of fostering good oral communication skills. The children I am currently working with are highly articulate and by and large confident and able, but interestingly, much of their energy and engagement arises from the fact they are thinking outside the box, challenging one another, being listened to in new ways and being under no pressure to be "correct" or "right".

Not much else to report on the home front. Andrew returned to Lagos today – we should see him within the fortnight for a day or two. The boys seem very much used to the coming and going now. Today was very seamless and unemotional. I hope they are not becoming indifferent.

Today was playgroup day but we didn't go as I wanted to be home to farewell Andrew and to speak with you. Playgroup is fun for the children and I enjoy it as it is very relaxing. Most of the mothers who attend now have only very young children; all the original old guard who I met five years ago have no one at home anymore. As a result, given that Tommy is child number three for me, I find I have very little to say about him (apart from to you – you are his Granny, after all) in these settings, and consequently find it hard to get into conversations. There can be an alarming tendency in parents to talk exclusively about their children. Maybe we are all like that in the first couple of years, before the banality hits home and the waking up feeling like it is *Groundhog Day* exhaustion sets in for good. Maybe that is the way of the world; but I somehow do not recall quite so much "baby talk" when Jack was an infant. Maybe I did not notice because I was so happy not having to go to work for those first few months. Or perhaps I was genuinely interested in burping techniques and good suppliers of organic nappies.

I appreciate that it is a rite of passage – having a child – and thus talking about it with like-minded people is all part of the experience. But when even the fathers seem more interested in their baby's digestive system and exploits at Gymboree than the state of the economy or the latest transfer from Arsenal, one begins to wonder whether one is in fact missing the boat.

It's not just playgroup of course; it's the playgrounds, school, coffee mornings, even sometimes at the workplace. I know you have said many times that you and the mothers of your generation never talked about us at all. I suspect you are glorifying some of those memories. You must have mentioned us in passing at some stage. I am sure I remember hearing about So and So's daughter who was so slim and a size 8, etc. I know that everyone had at least three or four children and so they were not particularly special – more taken for granted – if you like. But what *did* you talk about? Maybe this is one of those tales you tell that is not actually true, but which is designed to make me think that life was simpler and purer thirty years ago?

I have reflected on it quite a lot and I cannot generalise and say that women who work (or don't) are more prone to the long winded explanation of the minute and boring aspects of child-raising. There is no clear trend other than the extraordinary detail of the relevant tale and the glazed over eyes of the listener. Topics range from nap times and durations, night time waking frequency, eating habits, attitudes to homework, TV show preferences and behavioural foibles. Discussions can stray into the area of fathers of the child as well (often intriguing and entertaining, I grant you).

Behaviour issues can be quite interesting; especially naughtiness, rude words and funny remarks. The number and brand of nappies used and the contents thereof, less so. I do not mean to imply that I am critical of the interest people have in their children, and looking for the motivations behind these diverting conversations, I don't have to search long. I know that we all talk about what we are doing. I know that we are all bonding, trying to help if we can and looking for sympathy and connection with others. And sometimes a little bit of living vicariously or even boasting comes into it. It's like the chats over the fence in the suburbs. I think that what frustrates me though, is the fact that so often there *is* a real need underpinning the conversation; say a need to feel validated or a need to find an answer. While it is within my power to help a little bit, most often I don't because I sense that the answer or a suggestion is not really what they want to hear. They do not seem to want the problem to go away. But rather, in talking they satisfy the need to speak, to be heard, to assert their own place and point of view. It is as though the concern validates the speaker as a parent and the child as an entity.

I realise now, that in making that assumption, I am making myself unavailable for those who need to be listened to. A completely valid and valuable need, after all. Pretty bad form for a coach! I need to put this baggage aside and listen more carefully to discover the unspoken wish of the person in question.

Where there *is* a genuine concern that one wants input on, then clearly we all have or can find the solutions, if not within ourselves, then certainly within the peer group or the "village" we live in. There are literally scores of parenting websites and books at out finger tips, with all range of hints and support and references. Despite this people still discuss and query these same problems. It is not that the answers are out of reach. Could the expertise be more accessible? Could we be free from worry and stress and able to actually enjoy the situations that would otherwise be so vexing?

Would the market support yet another "How to.."?

I will start recording these chats between parents noting the main areas of concern. A cursory consideration suggests that diet, bathroom issues, behaviour and dealing with school, are key areas of interest. Based on that, I would collate a real person's guide to parenting. How would it be different from all that lies at our disposal already? Humour, for a start. Pocket sized and portable, or even an ebook available for down load on some snazzy ebook reader. For a title, I like "Purée, potties, princesses and poo – A guide to Parenting" or "Playground Politics – Cynical wisdom for parenting the under 8s".

The guide will cover the main needs of the infant; food, warmth, love. Then it willll move on to the growing child: play, independence, speech and so on. The key will be to keep it light; the market is saturated with serious tomes on how to feed, wean, potty train, teach, speak to and play with your child, addressing the scientific and psychological underpinnings of each. What we need is a method of getting the tried and tested wisdom of the woman (and man) in the street (suggestions though, not gospel truth) out to the general parenting public. Nothing too detailed or impenetrable.

One approach might be to set out the material by theme or topic. For example, under bathroom issues I would deal with potty training (no one is still in nappies when they start school – during the day, that is), how many poos are too many, and the intriguing process of classifying poo (with handy cross references to the Bristol Stool Scale and its seven types of poo). I would touch on the new mother's need to make time to wash and how to keep the bath white and importantly, when to see the dentist (the hidden evils of raisins at mass).

On getting help (not unsolicited advice) I would have to mention ways of encouraging Grandma to bite her tongue and supply a list of facial expressions designed to stop the know-it-all in their tracks. Entertainment and the value of boredom would be a big area e.g. cost effective birthday parties (or how not to spend £500 for the 2 year old's bash). And on behaviour I would highlight effective bribing strategies and discipline pitfalls. Another useful topic would be around language e.g. "swear words – alternatives".

Another piece would be the little tips for getting through red tape – like how to get an appointment at the doctor when the helpful receptionist insists they are fully booked, getting a place at a good school, and never queuing in the economy line when checking in for a long haul flight (most ground crew are either scared of or won over by the tenacious mother travelling alone with three small children). It will become a very useful miscellany for parents.

An alternative structure – perhaps easier to use – would be an alphabetical list of topics, with headings that capture the reality and which are not too bland.

This is what I have so far:

Abhorrence

A feeling of detestation or horror. This is not something to be ashamed of. These feelings can surface, or even explode, seemingly from nowhere, and without warning in a variety of situations. Sources of abhorrence include:

- changing the nappy of a child other than your own;
- some children;
- some parents;
- the nutrition details printed on the side of many kid oriented baked good;
- the cost of certain baby classes;
- returning to work before the child is sleeping though the night;
- vomit in the cot.

Accept that you are normal to feel like this and give yourself a break.

Alcohol

Men seem to think that children as young as 2 need to sample these substances. While disagreeing will mean you are seen as uptight, maintain a firm line on this one. The path to AA is paved with imbibing socialites who got the taste a little early... and sleep deprived mothers rewarding themselves once they get the bastards down of a night.

Anarchy

This is a state of extreme disarray in which, from time to time, children can flourish. Generally, however, too much will do your head in. Remember, the aim of the game is to come out happy and confident that you didn't ruin them entirely. Have a think about this if it is you who is thriving in the anarchy...

Argument

This form of disagreement and expression needs to be encouraged. Ideally, children should learn to manage the verbal ones without your help. This will require a lot of creativity and patience in the early years, especially with siblings. Girls of a certain age will test you again, but if the skills of debate and healthy disagreement are modelled form the start, there is a good chance your child will enter his teenage years knowing how to stand his ground, concede where beaten and use words, not fists. Having said all of that, you don't want to create experts whose skills leave you exposed and vulnerable. Also, be mindful of the fact that little jugs have big ears, and actions speak louder than words, before you get stuck into any massive marital blow up or a humdinger on the phone with your Mum.

Average

In spite of every hope and prediction to the contrary, no matter what you ate during pregnancy and no matter how soon you begin reading to him, in many respects, your child will end up average. No matter how early she says her alphabet, or how poised she is during her MMR vaccinations, chances are she will also be just plain ordinary at some things too. Accept this as soon as you can.

Axiom

There are few true axioms in parenting but the following precepts can be relied on:

- Economies of scale; more children means less work as they raise each other;
- More is less and less is more. Stand back and leave them to it sometimes; this develops imagination and resilience. Also note that the more effort you go to in the kitchen the more complaints of "uugh, disgusting!" you will hear.
- If you are hosting a dinner party they will repeatedly cry out, come out, or fall out, of their beds.
- No one likes a know-all.
- Girls like pink.

....

Questions

If there was one single area of parenting that you could prepare better for, it would be dealing with questions. If only the time spent mindlessly chewing the fat about Rachel in *Friends*, browsing in shops for another sweater or scarf and moaning on the phone about your job/mother-in-law/land-lord/husband, could be reclaimed and used for researching and stocking up data so that you could be ready with answers to the literally millions of questions they will ask you.

- What do turtles eat?
- Why do moths not look pretty?
- How many teeth does a shark have?
- What is onomatopoeia?
- Where is heaven?
- What is the difference between a crocodile and an alligator?
- Where does the Cat in the Hat go? And why does the children's mother leave them alone all day?

- Which dinosaur is this?
- What is radar?
- What is a logarithm?
- When will my lunch come?

I am thinking it would be a very big book actually – I seem to have a lot of material already. If it's too big and unwieldy it won't be marketable as the easy to use, quick solution, pocket sized guide I had in mind.

For now I should actually answer all of those questions above and set up a form on my website so that parents and children can submit more.

Anyway, please get some rest if you can and I will be in touch again soon.

Txx

2 October, 2008

Dear Mum,

I hope you are feeling a lot better today and that you had a decent night. We are all well. The weather has turned very cold and autumnal suddenly. Today was blustery and chilly, though mostly sunny. The second day of October and we have our winter coats on. It's always lovely when Autumn appears as if from nowhere. Even after a very cool summer, the sudden arrival of cold weather and darkening evenings brings a little frisson to the atmosphere. There is still novelty in the season change – even after 12 years. Almost a third of my life has been spent in the UK and I still get more excited by the impending winter than the promise of summer. Of course I will be singing a different tune by late November. Even all the over blown Christmas lights and excessive merriment, shopping and partying, will not distract me from the short grey days and the certain knowledge of three more months of gloom. But for now we are crunching and scrunching our way through the already voluminous piles of fallen leaves on the pavements feeling very joyful and "brrrish".

I received a very seasonal reception (chilly) when I arrived home today with Jack from school, after we had been at our afterschool activities. Felix was playing in the reception room and howled with misery at the sight of me, wailing that he did not want me home. He is loving spending more time - two afternoons a week with our nanny, Marta - that the very thought of me cutting short his fun had him in floods of tears. Meanwhile Tommy was being very rough and aggressive towards him as Felix was trampling on his special territory.

Marta is *his*, first and foremost. After a particularly wanton smashing of a car on Felix's head I said: "We don't use cars to hurt each other. And we don't kick. Where have you come from bringing this unacceptable behaviour?" he cogitated a moment and responded "India". Not to say that rough people come from India. But tigers do and no one messes with tigers.

We had another team meeting at work today. It was a long one – over 70 minutes. It occurred to me as my manager was relating events and tensions and current issues around the department that what the civil service needs is to equip each Department with a special internal agency or steering committee to guide it through the tough decisions, to lay down the law on difficult issues, to remove the risk of obfuscation and to actually know what the left and the right hands are doing at any given time.

I got quite carried away then, reflecting on the nature of such and wondering if I could suggest it to the "Innovation" people who look for new ideas to improve the department, the clients or the systems or to enhance the commercial wherewithal with which we operate (great alliteration, eh?).

I came up with the idea of creating a new departmental underscoring and development team (DUD) to be responsible for review and progress and all the other amorphous yardsticks and measures of civil service efficiency and fit for purpose client oriented smart and results driven working. Obviously, it would be focussed on Growth, Innovation and Transformation (GIT) while emphasising Progress, Reform, Originality and Development (PROD). It would be staffed by Leaders, Big Thinkers and Blue Sky Minds, not fearful of the Hard Calls, the Unpopular Decisions and the Tough Choices necessary to move the civil service forward and into a new era of productivity, optimism and opportunity (POO).

We would need Change Campaigners and Tenacious Teams of the Best, Brightest and Bravest Minds. From this platform we could strive to deliver the undeliverable, to unlock deadlocks, achieve resolutions, solutions, and where needed, begin revolutions. We would move towards movement of mountains, and raise the bar and even set a new standard for governmental excellence.

Such a far reaching and ambitious project would need clear parameters, prospects and purview. At the very least we would need new departmental cufflinks and ties emblazoned with the DUD logo and the GIT catchphrase. We could mint new coffee mugs, printed with the memorable strap line – "wake up and smell the ..." and then a variety of words could appear on the base of the mug, such as "changes", "new brew", "fresh air" (depending on grade and status of course) for the general amusement of the person sitting across from the mug.

We would then need to focus on the measures of progress towards our goals; the initial, interim, partially completed and mid-project review points. We would need buy in and commitment and ownership from our stakeholders, clients, strategic decision makers and relevant key personnel.

I was so excited about all of this that I then saw ways in which we might leverage the technology at our disposal. You know – take it into the e-world. I reckon we can develop some little faces (emoticons as they are known) to really sum up the experience at the heart of the GIT initiative. I am going to workshop and consult on that piece first, after I commission a costs analysis.

Assuming it is viable, we can move forward on developing the right images to use during and in assessing the key stages and steps of the GIT project. There are already a lot of emoticons we can use to convey expressions as to the status of our work e.g. the ubiquitous smiley face. There are also the following which would often be applicable I think - worried, nodding, shaking head, sleepy, bored, rolling on the floor laughing, nerd, smirking, secret telling, embarrassed and eye rolling – for which someone has taken the time to create an icon already.

But the most exciting part of what I envisage is that the DUD team, focussed on GIT, and working towards POO would be transforming government from the centre out, revolutionising our use and understanding of emoticons as a communication tool. In this era of accessible government, imagine the mileage to be gained from documents and consultations that cut through the verbiage and actually convey real meaning and depth of feeling. We will need our best IT resources and designers to come up with emoticons to convey the following:

- Pofaced
- Poncing
- Nonchalant
- Tepid
- Sitting on the fence
- Rushed off one's feet
- Obsequious
- Corruptible
- Lightweight
- Lost
- Uncomfortable due to overeating
- Hung over
- Hung out to dry
- Exposed
- Unemployed
- Beleaguered
- Demoralised
- Demotivated
- Head in hands
- Desperate
- Heavy of heart
- Hard of heart

- Lost heart
- Heart attack
- Suicidal

Read them again, slowly, and think of the little face that would be used to depict the state of mind or being in each case. Powerful, eh?

The only problem of course is that while a picture can paint a thousand words, I anticipate that most of the department will not be ready to move ahead on this swiftly and decisively. The process of choosing and agreeing on correct usage, typeface, colours, fonts, size and so on, will no doubt pose some logistical problems. Maybe we will need a green, white, blue and even pink paper analysing my idea, followed by some sort of high level dossier and pitch or presentation to the decision makers, then a sift and a cull of course. Oh and a public consultation with a steering committee and maybe even a...

Love you.

Tx

4 October, 2008

Dear Mum,

I was encouraged to hear today that your neutrophil and white blood cell counts were improving a little. Maybe this is the beginning of an end to the terrible discomfort and infections and the extreme tiredness. Fingers crossed.

We have just stepped in from dinner at a restaurant - or as Tommy calls it – west wan, which had me stumped for a while. It was lots of fun. We are all a little crazy now after a quiet, rainy day indoors. I followed through on my newfound interest to explore my artistic side and we all got into a little expression with colour today using acrylic paints and new canvasses. Tommy was occupied in the bath while we finished it off, as his idea of painting is to mess it all up as much as he can and then declare – "It looks like diarrhoea". It was pretty nice actually – a semi–abstract neo impressionistic naive Garden of Flowers.

All of our art will be of that genre. I should probably say all of *my* art will be that, as actually having lessons is a little beyond me right now. However, I did attempt a very therapeutic outpouring of blue and green last night which is now on the wall of my room – a seascape – storm at sea. I love creating the colours and layering them and seeing how it turns out. It is basically colour therapy and gives me a more immediate and less eye straining form of creative expression than cross-stitch and knitting. You have to admit I have done a lot of creative things in my time. Macramé, of course – which hardly counts, as who was not macraméing the glorious seventies away. Knitting and sewing. Admittedly, hand sewing without a pattern was never going to take me far. Then a lot of baking, the risotto years, scrapbooking, cross-stitch and tapestry. Have I kept my light under a bushel? Maybe if I had attended a school where more than three people in a year were allowed to be both academic and artistic, I might have discovered my gift sooner. Art was my one area of unexplored ability. We must have lumped it in with music. I am sure that music was more a question of application than wanton lack of talent. I know, I know – old Mrs Bungeon would disagree.

Anyway what does it matter? As long as the painting gives me pleasure, eh? Maybe I will send you a snap of my work.

I have not much other news to send you really. It is a shame to only write copious amounts when I have something to whinge about. I will sign off now and take up again soon. Keep your spirits up if you can, the 20 days of chemo and danger afterwards is more than half over now.

Tx

6 October, 2008

Dear Mummy,

I was thinking about you a lot today after we spoke this morning and you told me what a rotten day you were having. I wish I could be there. Of course I would love even more to take it all away from you and cure you, but your encouragement fell on deaf ears when we were choosing careers and there are no bloody doctors in the family. Lawyers are not much use at times like this. Though Claire's social work must be coming in handy.

I was at the boys' school today listening to the year 4 readers (as you might expect it was taking a herculean effort to get through some of their books – patience not being my strongest suit – but I found reserves I do not usually have for my own children) and I was reflecting on my childhood and all that you did for us – at school, with homework, playing, reading, talking. I was thinking this is what I want to write to Mum about – a note to let her know how much I appreciate all she ever did for me – and of course all you continue to do. Perhaps it is more poignant now that you are so ill and now that I have children of my own. But in any case it is long overdue that I tell you how much I cherish all my memories of you involved in my childhood experiences.

It is good for me to recollect these things. For one thing it reassures me that a time will come when my children will perhaps look back fondly on their childhoods and indeed, adulthoods, and be moved to express some pleasure or happiness regarding my role in that and hopefully, a recognition that I did not totally mess them up.

So Mum, thank you for reading with my year 2 class (and others – but year 2 is my strongest image). Thank you for the times you were on tuck-shop duty and you made me an extra special salad roll. I always recognised your writing on the brown bag. Thanks for reading to me so much and for cultivating and nurturing in all of us such an interest in books and speaking. To which end, thanks for all the help with debating and hearing my lines in drama. Thanks for the costumes as well. That Jesus/Saint Peter/unnamed Apostle red smock had a lot of use. Thanks for explaining to me that Rose in year 6 was probably jealous of me when she was mean and sarcastic and made jokes at my expense. Thanks for all the delicious birthday dinners when I could choose my favourite meal and we had coloured popcorn as an appetiser. Thanks for the fabulous Christmas presents that you kidded were from Santa, never revealing the truth til that horrible Mrs Cooper in year 4 made us do a project on Christmas where the research revealed he was "fictional". All those gifts were such fun, yet educational. Thanks for letting me see *Dot and the Kangaroo* with Dan and you, but also letting me be a "big kid" and go with Dad, Claire and James the same day to see *Star Wars* as well (must admit I did not understand any of it and still don't).

Thanks for keeping me honest and not colluding with me when I was mortified that I was graded a C in year 3 maths after doing really well in all the tests and feeling robbed of my rightful A or B. I tried to change the C to an A but you stopped me in time. Thanks for being fair and even-handed between me and the others, always making sure we "barred" or reserved the best things we savoured, like the crust on the unsliced bakery bread, the front seat of the car or the choice of book at bedtime. Thanks even, for so often telling me after spats with Dan, that I should have more sense, since I was older. While I hated it at the time and saw it as favouritism, it was probably true and did me no harm.

Thanks for always being available, fun and wise. Your humour and optimism and pragmatic common sense could be relied on to solve any problem – from what to wear to the myriad year 10 and 11 dances, to dealing with sunburn, to helping with homework, to getting Jack to gain weight and take a bottle as an infant.

Thanks for always saying "you got your brains from me", thereby ensuring that as a girl, I was proud and protective of my hard work and intelligence. Thanks for exposing me to England through the books and films we read and saw. *Chariots of Fire* captured my imagination and compelled me to the UK – a mixed blessing in many ways, but a wonderful experience and now a rich and interesting life.

Thanks for the chats over the years I have been away and for keeping me apprised of all the family's news, and for sharing my doings with them so that I was never a stranger on return visits. Thanks for pointing things out to me that I could not have seen so clearly on my own, such as – "you clearly get pleasure from your children", "you can't take criticism", "if you are going to have a career let's hope your children have a father who wants to stay home with them". I cherish your directness, even if sometimes not straight away!

There are countless other things that I appreciate, but I also want to apologise for a couple. First, I regret how rude I was to you when you gave me a Billy Joel cassette for my 14th birthday rather than Icehouse – only to find out later that you had arranged with my school friends not to give me Icehouse because they were doing so. I am also sorry for picking on your washing skills when you washed my lovely brown linen trousers in a warm wash and shrunk them. I could have washed them myself or had them dry-cleaned - I *was* 20 or so. But you were all apologies and never told me to go jump in the lake. I only realised later how much you loved the washing and the peace and respite the laundry could occasion.

Thanks for sharing things with me; your jewellery and handbags, recipes and ideas. Thanks for sharing some of your memories of the challenges of having a young family, making me feel far less isolated and incompetent, especially in the early days with a baby. Thanks for the advice; the undying interest and patience.

Above all, thanks for being such a selfless and, at the same time, self respecting person who modelled wonderful mothering behaviour, friendship and independence of mind and spirit. Thanks for showing me how to get on with things with positivity and humour. Thanks for letting me have a good vent about my frustrations or concerns; never letting them become huge issues or preoccupations. Thanks for encouraging me to fulfil my potential and not rest on my laurels. Thanks for always telling me I was lovely even when I wasn't – apart from telling me my face was thin and my features were like a rat's – but you just wanted me to put on weight.

Thanks for your sagacity and sanguinity. I know I have lots of good qualities that I have inherited from you and Dad but in recent years it is the capacity to laugh and remain optimistic that has served me best.

And finally, thanks for introducing me to *NCIS*, a perfect antidote to *West Wing* overload. Between that, some coaching, some painting and some reading my evenings are very full.

I apologise for typing this to you, but this way I can keep a copy of what I have said and remember again all these things. Maybe with the drugs you are on and the vision impairment they have occasioned the typeface will be easier to read than my scrawl, as well. Such a pity that your foray into psychedelic drugs is not a source of amusement.

I enclose some of the boys' drawings. Don't read anything into their subject – for some reason they decided to draw ballet dancers. Maybe they had you in mind and came up with a "girly" subject. They more often do planes and train maps and helicopters, though gardens and butterflies also feature heavily. Thankfully, not too much purple in evidence. They send you their love. Tommy is the same – rambunctious and charming and wilful. He is very considerate and always says "sorry Mummy" if I hurt my toe on a chair (always doing that) or sustain some other minor injury. He was very concerned about Jack's loose tooth which had him wailing at intervals all weekend. It finally fell out when I brushed his teeth for him, with no pain or bleeding. What a palaver. Admittedly, Jack paused to reflect when I pointed out that every single person in the world has or will have experienced this pain and that he can choose not to let it get him down quite so much. I wonder if hypochondria is a lifelong trait. The alarming thing is the learning from the *Seven Up* TV series and its premise: "show me a child at 7 and I will show you the man".

I hope this letter has not tired you out too much, and I hope that you begin to feel a little better with each passing day. All my love Mum, to you and Dad and all the family.

Tess x

9 October, 2008

Dear Mummy,

I am pleased that today was Thursday and so we had our weekly team meeting at the office.

Before I tell you about that; prepare for a scintillating episode of *Yes Minister* meets *Mr Bean* meets *Much Ado About Nothing*, I have to have a little vent.

At the school drop-off, I was wittily (I think) bemoaning the change of season and its impact on my wardrobe. I find it hard to get enthusiastic as winter approaches and one has to get out the woollens, and I was feeling frumpy and uncoordinated one day last week, commenting to a very elegant Spanish mother of three that I need a new look. I was overheard by another lady who told me I was fine – I just look like a mum. While that is not a bad thing – it was not intended as a compliment.

Given that four mornings each week I am in work shoes, tailored trousers or skirt and jewellery with a smart top, I wondered where that remark came from. Admittedly on my day off I am dressed in jeans or casual pants and t-shirt with gym shoes – as I am on the way to the gym from school. What exactly does it mean to "look like a mum"?

I let myself go along with it and I was then told that really good quality jeans and a blazer should be the centrepiece of my wardrobe. I was impressed with the certainty of the opinion. I am always a little uncomfortable in jeans it has to be said, the fabric is not smooth or soft or easy to work in, or walk in, the zipper and button bits are hard on the old midsection and despite every utterance to the contrary they are in essence, casual. Also, one cannot wear denim to conferences with senior members of the tax bar.

So after some reflection I daresay I am back where I started from. All the people over the years who have told me I look good, even elegant, can't be colluding to make a fool out of me can they? So one day a week I look like a "mum"? Well, that's what I am. Will a pair of yellow plimsolls convince the world that I am not a mum? No, just that I am not happy being one.

Back to the office. I have revolutionised my way of working. Instead of trying not to rock the boat and never say or write anything without due prior consideration, vetting and checking that what I have said will not offend, I have committed to myself to be more authentic at work. And so today I sent an email asking one of my colleagues at another office an ostensibly innocent, but actually very dumb, question. I should have known the answer or found it out. By writing down such a question and copying it to a lot of people I revealed:

a) My ignorance. One should never do this; not ever at work, unless young, really pretty and slim and single.

b) My political naïveté. Not finding out pecking orders and protocols is almost as bad as ignorance.

c) I appear not to care about A) and B). This lack of care may be the worst thing, and not caring in a semi public forum like an email to colleagues and superiors is tantamount to giving up on one's career.

I have found a very good way to look upon my time in the office though. Apart from the obvious amusement and stimulation the work and people provide, the copious quantity of art work adorning the walls is truly inspirational. Given my new found interest in painting, I am very keen to explore the bowels and heights of the building to gaze upon the many works that brighten its halls and corridors.

Did I tell you that I am off to Paris this weekend for a "24 hours before sunset" experience with my old mate Helen? She and the family are staying in the 7th Arrondisement and as I have Andrew back this weekend I have secured leave from the boys to join them for a night and most of the following day. It will be lovely. I embark from the new Eurostar terminal at Kings Cross St Pancras after a glass of champagne at the world's longest champagne bar – getting me in the mood for an evening on the tiles with Helen and Harry. It's more than four years since I was last in Paris – that time with Claire. We spent a memorable day tripping through Le Marais, the Left Bank, the 6th and sampling coffee after coffee until we contrived to rest with a Campari in the shadow of the Eiffel Tower, after a jaunt around the Musée D'Orsay.

Anyway I am very excited at my night away and the prospect for some Parisian relaxation, walking along the Seine, sampling the art and the ambiance. Maybe given the recent wisdom concerning my appearance I can use the trip as a way to reinvent myself – buy the jeans?

The office is surveying its clients to assess the quality of our service.

I would love to have that job.

Maybe alongside or as part of my coaching offering I could offer a service of conducting surveys and questionnaires – bespoke and tailor made to elicit the valuable insights you cannot seem to gather any other way. Clients embarking on a really transformational process might want to use a questionnaire themselves or seek feedback from their friends and colleagues through one.

For example, I could uncover the views of everyone the client has ever worked with, befriended, pissed off or annoyed in anyway. Ensuring anonymity would guarantee honest and fulsome responses. The Surveyee would feel free to let rip and vent their spleen. Meanwhile, the client could use the feedback to facilitate a process of discovery and personal growth. I might commission someone to do handwriting analysis so that while anonymous, the answers could be sifted and sorted according to just what sort of person they were given by.

For example: A Type aggressive, competitive, high achievers tend to find you a simpering wimpish drip. Women hate you because you don't seek their approval. It would be taking things to a new level of honest and direct and ideally, timely, feedback, and it would be unique, in that it would cross over into the personal, rather than merely professional, realm.

I know it seems brash, but who doesn't have a self indulgent and morbid curiosity about what the ex- boyfriend or ex-boss or former flatmate really thought of them? What the best friend would like to say now, what the husband thinks when he doesn't think you will find out the thoughts are his? It would be very empowering and liberating to have all of that stuff out there.

There would be risks. Like any personal growth journey there could be emotion and setback, even violence and depression. But that only brings further opportunities to me as Coach. I could have various survey points in the process of coaching. Say, at an early stage we could assess whether the client would really benefit from a survey. A pre-survey questionnaire, if you like, starting with a very bland and gentle process, where the client takes a questionnaire to find out whether to solicit feedback from third parties. The next step would be a questionnaire to sort out the nature of the feedback they might benefit from (e.g. in my case, fashion advice), then a choice of surveys for the actual third parties to fill in.

Then, in the case of eliciting the views of third parties, I could cast some questions very openly to welcome broad feedback or narrowly to force them to say what the client wants to hear. I think there would be a lot of demand for the latter style. The Surveyee would not be aware they are being led if I could make the questions clever enough.

It would be very niche, of course. Only really robust clients would be looking for the information in the first place, but from among that group one could find some great potential for change. A pithy name and really good marketing could deliver huge results.

In the case of clients looking to clarify their own views on themselves, not needing third party input, a range of topics could be surveyed. For example:

What colour kitchen do I really want?
When is it too late to leave home?
Am I an alcoholic?

Then the responses could be analysed and presented:

Khaki prevails.
If you have to ask...
Read it and weep.
Sort out your own shit first.
Face the music.

The beauty of being skilled in this arena is that virtually no area is off limit. Somehow, a series of questions on a piece of paper is less threatening than an actual person asking the same things. The Survey amounts to a virtual coach. The client is asked perceptive and challenging questions that raise their awareness. In answering honestly (price may determine that), the client is confronted by those "aha" moments of revelation which could catalyse change or action.

Obviously a huge market already exists in the arena of relationship advice. Magazines are full of quizzes aimed at finding the right partner, improving relationships or spotting when the relationship is over. Maybe it's time for a questionnaire that puts the horse before the cart though. Maybe the singles need a device to help them assess whether a relationship is really for them at all.

Bear with me here because I am thinking as I write.

How's this:

Spring to Mind Coaching
Questionnaire for the Lovelorn

1) Are you looking for love in the right places?

a) Is there a right place?
b) If I knew that I would not have asked for help!
c) Yes. There is nothing wrong with *me*.
d) No, I am hopeless in this regard and have no way of knowing what to do or where to look.
e) I'm not really looking but if someone nice happened to come along that would be a bonus.

2) Where do you think Mr or Mrs Right is right now?

a) Probably having a great time doing something really interesting.
b) There is no such person.
c) Looking for me.
d) Married to someone gorgeous, on holiday in Capri.
e) No idea.

3) What is your best relationship memory?

a) I have several.
b) I have none.
c) My fabulous outfits when we went to hip clubs.
d) Having someone special to cherish and to complete me.
e) Spending quality time with my family.

4) What is your worst relationship memory?

a) The stage when you know it is coming to an end.
b) I have none.
c) That sinking feeling when I realise I am wasting my time on a big dud.
d) The arguments, the cheating, the screaming, the stalking, the break-ups. I can go on?
e) Being made to feel less important than his work and friends and other interests.

5) On a scale of 1-10, describe your ideal mate in terms of his or her money earning potential.

a) 7
b) No idea. Not high if it means I will not find anyone.
c) 10
d) 8. I'm not buying his beer and cigarettes.
e) 2. I will have my family's support.

6) On a scale of 1-10, describe your ideal mate in terms of his or her looks and dress sense.

a) It's very subjective and depends on the whole package.
b) Beggars can't be choosers.
c) 10
d) Bastards are always good looking.
e) 4 – but it also depends on what my family think.

7) On a scale of 1-10, describe your ideal mate in terms of his or her sense of humour.

a) 9

b) No idea. Not high if it means I will not find anyone.

c) 7 – as long as he is not funnier than me.

d) 4. *American Pie* is not funny.

e) 7 - but he needs to really appreciate my family's jokes and stories.

8) On a scale of 1-10, describe your ideal mate in terms of his or her family mindedness.

a) 7-8.

b) No idea. Not high if it means I will not find anyone.

c) 3. Not interested in Mummy's boys.

d) 6. Bastards never want a family.

e) 11, though that is my family primarily. And he must want lots of kids.

9) Of the following, which category of men would you tend to prefer:

a) George Clooney, Gregory Peck, William Holden and the characters they play.

b) Anyone will do.

c) As long as he is a banker, loaded, drives a sports car or is a photographer, film director, agent, celebrity, plastic surgeon, oil tycoon or ex of a model, I am not fussy.

d) Up and coming sportsmen, musicians, artists... but ad execs are ok.

e) Doctors, lawyers, accountants.

10) What kills the romance for you?

a) Self satisfied and self important monologues.

b) Nothing.

c) Him looking at other women.

d) His flat/house and his mates.

e) His need for his mother's approval.

11) Of the following list of leisure pursuits which would you happily cultivate if it meant finding a mate?

a) Golf, sailing, viticulture, hill walking, wine tasting.

b) Absolutely anything, except snooker, chess and watching *Dad's Army*.

c) Race car driving, polo, pole dancing, life drawing, cigars, yachting.

d) Cricket, tennis, battle re-enacting, clubbing, running marathons.

e) Picnicking, dry-stone walling, volunteerism.

12) How would you rate your chance of finding love if you continue doing what you have always done?

a) Pretty good. You never know what might be around the corner.

b) It doesn't matter what I do; love is not for me.

c) Great, what I really need are tactics to keep him long enough for me to get maintenance.

d) Not high. Love is elusive and I will not find it easily.

e) Very good. I just need to focus on it.

13) If you could change five things about yourself in order to enhance your chances of finding love, what would they be?

a) My job, my haircut, my tendency to be too critical, my self-sufficiency, my fear of flying.

b) Only five??!

c) That's hard; my expensive tastes... the cosmopolitans every day...the nicotine... the stalking ex-girlfriend.

d) My age, my history, my propensity to love bastards and commitment-phobes, my refusal to accept the help of my friends, my clinginess.

e) My lack of experience, my naïveté, my obsession with family, my premature judgements about potential partners, my closed mindedness.

What do you think? It is ready to use, applies to many sorts of potential client and does not need a long winded explanation.

Stage two for the Lovelorn might be a survey aimed at discovering the hidden and unspoken views of friends. It could be very revealing. Who better to provide advice than the poor, beleaguered, ear bashed friends who have been through it all alongside the Lovelorn? If they had the protection of an "official" questionnaire to hide behind (and the guarantee of anonymity), with questions that conceal, rather than expose their identity, then the client could benefit greatly from the honest feedback. Imagine the power of finally ripping back the layers of self deception and denial and finding strategies to overcome the problems that the questionnaire identifies.

My main challenge would be assessing the client's appetite for candour as opposed to spin and obfuscation, or lies that boost the ego. I will need to hone my listening skills and hear the client's unspoken wish in commissioning me to conduct the survey and follow up work. Depending on the raw data of course, I might have a difficult job re-casting the suggestions in a constructive way, but I think the coaching training will really help me there, not to mention my time in the civil service. This might finally give me the opportunity to savour, rather than resent the obligation (albeit, self imposed) to be diplomatic. Such a worthwhile and helpful role to play.

What do you think of this:

Client says:	Survey says	Coaching Approach 1 "Hands-off"	Coaching Approach 2 "Directive"
Men just don't notice me.	You are fat and plain.	Think about your appearance and consider dressing for your body shape.	Join a gym, go on a diet and wear some make-up.
I always go for complex men with a lot of baggage.	You only like freaks that no-one else can endure.	Is there some part of you that wants to rescue the stray? Shall we work on that?	Look for simple, straight forward men who look you in the eye. Meanwhile, stop believing you are unlovable.
There really are no good ones left.	There are plenty of men - you are a snob who will only settle for a surgeon or an investment banker.	Let's reconsider what you mean by "good"?	You will get what you deserve with that attitude.
I just can't be bothered getting out there.	You are lazy and lack ambition.	And where will that take you?	What? You think anyone will find you at home in this spinster's pad, this floral prison, this bastion of female self-limitation?

I only go for bastards.	You love being the victim and love the attention it brings you.	If he is a bastard what does that make you? Do you what to be that person anymore?	Grow up and take a good hard look at yourself. It is time to stop this narcissistic attention seeking.
I absolutely refuse to be matched up.	You are too proud to let anyone you know help you.	Ok. We can leave that alone and find another way. This is your quest after all.	Let's talk about your need for control, your refusal to be vulnerable and your resentment of people who have what you want.
I will never be so desperate as to use speed/internet /agency dating.	You are in denial about how desperate you are.	People have always relied on intermediaries to help them find love. Look at Austen's Emma. Let's explore the more modern methods and options before we eliminate them.	If it gets you some dates, what's the problem?

I can imagine that it is hard for you to get too excited about all of this. If you had lived in the UK for 12 years though, you might understand that the "honesty is the best policy" tenet is not taken as seriously here as it is in Australia. Also from where you are placed in an oncology ward this must all seem very trite and irrelevant. I am mindful of that Mummy, and I do not want to be insensitive.

I will sign off and let you rest dear Mummy.

All my love.

Tx

10 October 2008

Dear Mummy,

I was reminded today of that old quip you used to make at traffic lights when the car in front stayed stationary for ages after the light turned green. Do you remember? You always said: "People are not very intelligent". Finding other examples is not hard. I was in a shop today and the customer ahead of me was paying with a card and had to enter her pin. She was with her young daughter and the child – all of three – was pestering her to press the buttons on the machine. The mother picked her up and said: "of course my sweet little pumpkin, you are Mommy's best helper, you must do the numbers. Show everyone how smart you are and how you know all your numbers. Press 8728 and then the green button. Well done. You are a princess. Yes you can have a candy."

Yesterday at the gym pool a father, enjoying his swim with his sons, aged around 4 and 2, was tossing them into the water, from heights above his head, face first towards the edge. It was excruciating and I had to leave mid-swim. I swear he will lobotomise those poor little pets.

It was wonderful to hear your voice sounding so strong this morning and that you are feeling much better today. It is very reassuring that your blood tests are showing such an improvement in the white cell and neutrophil levels. We are all hoping very much that you have turned the corner now and will only be on the mend from here on.

As I mentioned, I am off to Paris tomorrow. There was much wailing and gnashing of teeth in the boys' room at bedtime last night when I told them, foolishly. I persuaded them they would hardly notice given Daddy would be back.

I told Bridget I was going, in an email in response to her excited news of her imminent trip to Central and South America. She responded as follows:

"Paris. Wow! How decedent of you!"

She then asked why Helen was in Paris in the first place. I think she was implying that no one else should be taking trips at this time of year. Maybe we are all very decedent to be travelling because we have children and people such as us should not escape to exotic destinations.

I was a little lost for words – again. I wanted to say all sorts of things – but emails are notoriously ambiguous when one tries to communicate in tense situations. I went with the option of being sincere and answered that Helen is on a family holiday. And made no remark about how *decedent* I am.

I am now mulling over my general decadence.

I know she meant decadent. The online thesaurus – just so we are in no doubt here – gives me alternative meaning such as degenerate, depraved, immoral, self-indulgent, sinful and wanton. I explored some of those synonyms further and found myself to be thus, sybaritic, effete(!), hedonistic, dissolute and debauched.

I then had to consider which part of my going away for a night was so reproachful. Was it the short nature of the break, the fact it is in Paris, the fact that it is *me* going or the wanton lack of responsibility I will thus have for the children and husband who, after all, I have no meaning without?

Then I thought maybe it was not a spelling error after all. Perhaps she did mean decedent. I am dead to many people I know, and huge parts of me died some time ago, but to associate Paris with death seemed unnaturally gloomy.

So it must be that she was saying "decent" – in the congratulatory ra-ra way of a PG Wodehouse character – "Jolly decent of you old girl." Perhaps she meant how "deserved". Or how delightful or how decided or even how Dedede (a character in Nintendo computer games).

I think, on balance she meant decedent after all. I would have to be dead to get a break from the children.

Tx

October 12, 2008

Dear Daniel,

Wonderful to speak to you today and hear all your news.

Was very concerned to hear from Mum that the next step is a biopsy to help the doctors decide whether to do further chemotherapy or whether to stop – i.e. give up. What became of the remission option? All the websites said that was what the induction chemo was aimed at. There was no giving up mentioned? I am not happy with this list of options and not really coming to this party, sorry. I have been stoically managing a very cheerful denial and that is most definitely what I intend to keep doing. When they do that biopsy I am going to jolly well have a look at the results and check their work for myself. All this giving up and not bothering talk, as if it's some midterm spelling test or an under 10's touch ruby game in the F division (you remember).

It's not good enough. After all those nasty side effects and all of our prayers and hopes and wishes and sending of positive thoughts and uplifting messages, I am just not going to accept anything other than a complete remission.

And now poor Mummy is lying there in that bed, awaiting the biopsy result, like a death row prisoner waiting for the Governor's pardon, with dear Dad by her side keeping his vigil. What else can they do though? It's horrid. I am firmly convinced that pragmatic positive good thinking combined with a good chunky dose of denial has got us this far. Why give up now?

I should not even be writing this down. It is unkind and insensitive and mere words can't really deal with the range and depth of emotions racing through the whole family. I have not been there and seen the real impact of the treatment or the toll on Mum and Dad and you. I have not heard the coughing or wheezing or helped her to the bathroom, or watched her struggling to sit or talk or sleep. I really cannot make any comment other than – no bloody way am I giving up on her!

Having said that I was checking airfares to see when and how I can get there. If this is it I am not doing it long distance.

I have to stop for a bit, the denial is giving way to a little emotion. I will return later, after a bit of distraction therapy…

It is now the evening. I finally got the boys to be quiet and stop revving one another up. Tommy is the main culprit as he has had a day time nap and he just keeps fooling around keeping the other two awake. I was on the phone with my "coach" - a colleague from the coaching course and she could hear the boys being so loud - screaming and laughing - and I was calling out threats that the dragon lady (me with appropriately fierce and fiery voice and expression) would be coming if they did not stop.

They have a special "phonedar" hardwired into their brains. Think of dogs picking up very high pitched sounds. Children can hear and sense when their mother is on the phone, even through several rooms and closed doors, so that no matter what they are doing and no matter how immersed in it they are, 5 minutes into a phone call they are all at the feet of the mother demanding any or all of a drink, help with their game, attention or assistance breaking up a fight or retrieving a toy. Not only do they come and hang around and make lots of noise, but they also harangue and harass and demand things while you have your hand up saying –"I am on the phone, five minutes". It is so sick and perverse that I can only explain it as a basic instinct right up there with self preservation and the perpetuation of the species.

Interestingly, it only applies where the mother figure uses the phone. When the father's phone rings children instantly quieten down and respectfully leave the room.

In any case, the call with my coach was helpful as I was able to discuss the options for getting down to Australia in the coming weeks and how to manage the children if I should go. If Andrew can't get back here for a week straight then I shall have to take them all with me – whatever the cost financially and emotionally of having them there with me – it won't be as huge a toll as the cost to me personally if I don't get there soon.

I know that this is giving up talk. When I began this letter I was not prepared to accept that I might need to rush over there. But seven hours is a long time some days. So no it's not that I am assuming the worst will have come to pass with the biopsy – but I am preparing for all exigencies. If I have to take the boys out of school, book airfares and rent an apartment in Brisbane, then so be it. I am not going to not see my Mum and all of you at this terrible time. If nothing else it is a time to be with my family, not alone here wondering whether now is an ok time to call.

On top of all of that, I am now getting a cold. All my late nights writing and working on my coaching websites and contracts are catching up with me – oh, and my night in Paris over the weekend. As Mum always said to me after I had children "You pay for your pleasure". Indeed you do.

It seems that more often than not, any sort of break or treat is followed by a minor misfortune. This time I broke my glasses in Paris. If I get a babysitter and eat out I usually spend the following day ill – either the cold air does me in or I catch a tummy virus (not alcohol poisoning on one glass). It is truly pathetic.

Anyway, I did have a lovely time in Paris. I was reading a newspaper without interruption during the outward journey. It is months since I read a Saturday paper. They are so dense, with so many different sections. I usually throw away gardening, motoring, money and travel straight away on the grounds that I cannot do the first to save my life, I am bored senseless by the second and third and can't go anywhere anyway as regards the fourth. That leaves books, art and film, style and news – which actually I have to admit usually offer nothing of interest either. Some weekends I only manage to read the TV guide.

This trend finally forced me to stop wasting my time and money, and the trees. At the Eurostar terminal I bought a paper though, because WH Smith was giving a free bottle of water away with each one. I read the sections of interest in a most relaxed and concentrated fashion and stepped off the train so much wiser. Shall I summarise my findings – or rather what stayed with me? I should preface this by saying that while in Paris Helen introduced me to a journalist friend of hers living there, who asked me what I thought "the story was with Gordon Brown". Clearly, nothing else about me or London was of interest to her. Being a journalist (from Brisbane) her intent was to discuss the press on him, so I said: "With all due respect, I don't bother reading the papers as the coverage is typically either biased, misinformed or sensationalist."

I can't remember whether I formed the impression that she was not very interested in me before or after I said that.

Nevertheless, the things I learnt from my free paper were as follows:

1. The credit crunch is going to have long felt cataclysmic effects across the globe.
2. There are bargains to be had for some – if you have some cash and know what you are looking for.
3. Chief executives are to blame for the financial woes facing the world.
4. Taxpayers will prop up the banks.
5. Keane have a new album out.

6. Britons love austerity and deprivation so there is some joy to be felt at the grim times ahead.
7. There is a whole new market to be made in style during lean times.

As regards 7 above, I was delighted to learn all the ways in which I can maintain a "champagne lifestyle on a cava budget" (*Marie Claire*). The paper quoted several well known figures citing the best thing about a recession. These range from making do with soup and homemade food, to having to read a book and play board games for amusement. Let's see how many articles like that are printed a year from now, when the banks are bust and the bread queues resemble those of Soviet Russia.

Consider the newsprint and paper that will be expended to sell magazines and newspapers replete with archived photos of depression era chic a la 1931, advice on how to exude style when skint and what not to wear during a recession. The Food section will be full of recipes aimed at extracting five meals out of one chicken (the buttery at Downing College has been doing that for donkeys years), Travel will glorify Blackpool and Features will consist of upbeat stories of triumph in adversity.

Now I know I am not that well-placed to criticise the media, given that I do not read a range of papers or magazines and I do not watch very much TV news. However, what little I am exposed to seems to have made a lot of copy out of promoting flagrant consumerism and wanton expenditure, hedonistic travel and self indulgent luxury spa treatments, issue after issue after issue, for the past decade. Will we now have to endure self congratulatory claptrap about shopping for less, mending and making do and amusing the children on a shoestring? Does the media form or reflect public sentiment?

The glory days of the noughties will now be passé and vulgar.

We've all been shunning plastic bags for a while of course, but now we can find new uses for all of our cast off clothes and in particular last season's high street purchases (you see, I also read that one does not keep anything from H & M for more than one season).

This is the banal, the mediocre, the trite and the insulting at its best. You know, until the column space was dedicated to it I had no idea one could swap clothes with someone, or donate to a charity shop or even, God forbid, not actually shop in the first place for another coat, pair of Killer Heels or lash lengthening mascara, advertised by models wearing fake lashes (as described in the small print at the foot of the page). I know we are presumed to be stupid, overpaid, undiscerning and lacking in taste and judgement, but are we also sheep? Perhaps we are. Apparently the market turmoil is purely driven by the group think and herd mentality.

All of this energy and effort now put into this new area of expertise – how to make do in hard times. The press portrays this as wisdom, alchemy. The readers cannot do anything without first reading about it in the Saturday papers, and they cannot feel confident about anything unless they are told that Brad Pitt, Posh or Gwyneth is doing it.

Just wait. My prediction is that soon we will see a huge credit crunch inspired uplift in church attendance as people get "back to basics" and rediscover their community and the "source". It will be chi-chi to have your home repossessed and to shop at Oxfam, provided you have last year's Manolos, the right colour ugg boots and the *Vogue* prescribed "less is more" hair and lipstick.

I am going to jump on the bandwagon and beat them to it. I will start a column on the local on-line mother's forum offering advice to help women make do.

- How to wash and go – Hair on the edge.
- Feed your family on £2.50 a day.

- Second hand everything – handbags, teabags, holidays, husbands.
- Recycle it – sheets, shoes, and shampoo bottles.

I reckon we can fuel an economic recovery by saving our money and not buying the newspaper – also saving the forests – and instead using common sense – my goodness – and just finding something apart from shopping to keep us amused. What will this nation of shopkeepers – hah – do if they cannot afford to shop? Read, talk, smile at someone? Oh they will still have football. Maybe women supporters' numbers will increase as they find they can no longer justify Saturdays on the high street and at the salon. Mind you the audiences will all be relying on free to air TV for their fix, as no one will be able to afford tickets or digital coverage...

Thankfully my world will not greatly change. I might buy fewer cappuccinos, cut back on the expensive out of season fruit and the bone crushing reflexology.

And given my complete lack of style I am going to set new standards in cheap and cheerful fashion with a new look around Kensington. Mens' flannel pjs under my boots and old coat, with ribbed tights like we wore at school (so warm). I will wear old socks as hats, scarves and gloves. I will reuse tins and wrappers over and over for storage, carrying receptacles and boho jewellery. It will be the new "homeless couture". The recession's answer to heroin chic and floral grunge.

But seriously, think about the social upheaval that lies ahead in modern Britain, if not in the developing world and beyond. What about the luxury car market, the models, the couturier houses, real estate, holiday hotels and air travel. And the gourmet food halls? Ripping us off unceremoniously for a few grains of barley and a sprig of broccoli (or rather, brocolini and bocconcini)? What about the private school fees, the extracurricular activities, the gym memberships?

We will be thinner from walking and less bocconcini (67% calories from fat). We won't be able to afford cars. We will have no cash for indulgent treats or expensive wine. Childhood obesity a thing of the past? The mind boggles. The air will be cleaner, the roads emptier, shops will close for want of business. Lidl will expand and outstrip the expensive Tesco. Waitrose will become so squeezed that it will sublet space to farmers to sell direct to the public, minus all the packaging and plastic shopping bags that fuelled so much snobbery among certain middle class women in the 90s, who would not be caught dead carrying their library books/knitting/lunch in any old plastic bag. The tubes will empty as hundreds of thousands return to their own shores.

At last I will discover the Britain of my dreams....

Tx

October 14, 2008

Dear Andrew (skpe message)

Hope Washington meetings are progressing well. Glad the weather is fine. Freezing here too.

I knelt on my glasses while in Paris and they are all bent out of shape. All attempts to get them back into order have only made them worse so that now I feel as if I am wearing someone else's specs. I am getting a headache from the eye strain and generally feeling other worldly as a result. If I had not gone to Paris I would never have knelt on my specs. The frustration and self loathing have undone all the benefits of the mini-break.

Spoke with Dad last night. It seems that Mum's biopsy today is to determine the progress of the blasts after the chemo. If they have been reduced from over 20% levels to under 5% they regard that as positive and will do another round of chemo – to consolidate. If they are not below 5% they will not – it is not working.

How awful. Fingers and legs and everything crossed that the levels are less than 5% though even so, the prospect of more chemo can't be enticing. Can you give some thought to when you can be in London for a working week and the weekends either side?

Dad tried to sound calm and self possessed but we shared several silences and it was all a little fraught. They are praying furiously. As am I. I have an open line going I think. It's like having the wireless broadband switched on and the laptop powered up all day. I am instant messaging and it's easier than normal, because God is never

116

offline or busy, or blocking access to me. Let's hope He is feeling inclined to acquiesce to our pleas.

Xx

October 14, 2008

Dearest Claire,

I am thinking of you all at the moment and know that you are all just waiting by Mum's side. I wish I were there. I was up late last night looking at cancer resources on the web. There is a brilliant website from a cancer institute in the US[3] which gives comprehensive yet comprehensible information on the different types of leukaemia, treatment and prognosis. It also covers grief and depression and coping issues for both the patient and the family. It was comforting to know that millions of people experience all of this every year. They even listed the 4 stages of grief[4]. One likes to know one is normal I guess.

After digesting all of that information I could conclude that I have moved out of denial into pre-emptive grief. Part of that is that one can feel a little removed from the ill person as one tries to cope with their potential loss. I suppose that is I why I am writing to you or with you in mind – rather than to Mum. One can hardly write to her and download one's thoughts about being the daughter of a cancer sufferer.

Having spoken to Dad I also feel that the phone is dreadfully inadequate for dealing with the things one wants to say. I am just living in the hope that it is all understood and that our familial bond will ensure that the things I want to say can be inferred from the fact I called.

---

3 National Cancer Institute – www.cancer.gov
4 An interpretation of Psychiatrist Elizabeth Kubler-Ross's work in identifying five stages of grief in her seminal work On Death and Dying (1969) - denial, anger, bargaining, depression and acceptance. More recent interpretations include Dr Phil – "Newer research and my own experience tell me that, really, there are not stages of grief but an array of feelings that arise"; Real Life: Preparing for the 7 Most Challenging Days of Your Life.

How are you going? I imagine you are well and truly over the denial phase as well, or perhaps in a selective denial pattern? Switching into it for work and shopping and walking into the ward. I am praying that I can get there to see you all soon. It is pretty awful sitting here powerless and imagining the worst. Not that you would have much power either, but at least you are all together and just giving her a cuddle or smoothing her brow would be something to do at least.

The thing about moving out of denial and into semi acceptance and pre-emptive grief is that one has no time for all the distractions that one was relying on during denial, one disdains and disowns those old coping mechanisms and with the new found perspective feels resentful of such trite and meaningless concerns, in the face of life's huge challenges. The worries about whether I am mumsy in appearance or whether I am decadent/decedent? Seriously, what was that all about? A sad and desperate attempt to distract myself from the reality lurking just ahead of us.

I am thinking of Mum and Dad all the time. I spoke with Mum for a couple of minutes this morning and she said how wonderful you and Dad have been, and Dan and James too. You are Claire.

Much love

Tx

October 15, 2008

Dear Claire,

Sing Hosanna, eh? Feeling ebullient and overjoyed at the news that Mum has responded so well to the chemo. They found no leukaemia and she may even go home in a few days! Thanks so much for sending me the update by text. What a relief. She and Dad must be overjoyed. She can have a little bit of semi-normal convalescence before the next round of chemo starts. I cannot begin to express my relief.

I had a lovely relaxed day with Tommy today. I was trying to keep busy and not be too anxious waiting to hear from you or Dad so we went to the Tate Modern Gallery and saw an installation of a giant spider with its legs spanning rows of blue and yellow metal bunk beds. I applaud the recycling rationale and the creative use of the large space, but... having a newfound interest in art has not given me an appreciation for the merits of installations such as that. I was unable to "get it". Could I create such a work and become an overnight success? Indeed. "After breakfast at my place" would be a good theme for an installation. I could create massive bread crumbs and milk slops and cornflakes ground up by feet – strewn over a floor of smeared and cracked tiles, with a loud speaker blasting a recording of my voice yelling: "Would you come and brush your teeth now". Now that is art.

In a similar vein I could create a monster sized toilet with a few dots of yellowish pretend wee on the rim, next to a big bath with bluish fake saliva showing the aftermath of the tooth brushing phase.

If I could do it all at a size of maybe 6-10 times the real thing, it could have real impact.

Then I could do an installation of how I feel during my work day. I would create massive 3D letters and coats of arms of Her Majesty's Government (might need permission for that), interspersed with Illy coffee cups and large red tin foil wrappers (chocolate). There would be a Daliesque clock sliding over a copy of the tax legislation, flowing down over a knife edge with the impression of scores of little grey men on it. Then I would have a projector beaming the image of a very complex tax structured financing idea – a diagram of the cash flows and the various corporate entities involved, with little illegible annotations peppered over it. It would all be lit under a very dull grey lighting scheme. I might also incorporate the big wee drops into this piece as well, given their abundant supply in the disabled toilets in my wing of the building. I am not being unkind with that observation, as the only users of those facilities are all able bodied men, and me – though only once.

I could go on. But the depth of feeling and meaning in my proposed giant art works would convey so much more than the large spider, or dare I say it – an unmade bed.

What makes these things art? Is it just about creating something to fill the space? If so, then open it up to the rest of the population to come up with something inspiring.

I wrote to you that all of the trivial sources of distraction during the denial phase cease to divert one during the stages of semi-acceptance and pre-emptive grief. Having said that, I found myself today at the customer service desk at the supermarket complaining that the yoghurt we buy - a four pack of organic fruit flavours - has been mispriced on the shelves for over 2 weeks; costing me 36 pence more than I expected to be charged. I hasten to add that it's not the money that had me standing there, but the principle. It took 20 minutes to be refunded 48p for the 3 packs I had bought under this false impression (she was feeling sorry for me and gave me more than she should have). Then she gave me a free pack by mistake. A saving of a huge £2.06. So if I value my time at the princely sum of £6 pounds/hr, it was time well spent.

They were running a travelling book sale at school today. For every book sold a book is donated to the school library. I had an interesting conversation with one of the mums helping to sell the books. She felt it was wrong for children to be consuming and spending all the time and in really unnecessary ways. I had to refuse Jack another book, a day after buying him one that he has barely opened. They come to expect new things all the time if not managed; last week it was a lanyard (a nerdy thing's that one attached one's office security card to and wears around one's neck) that he wanted. I ended up telling him that money did not grow on trees, that each book sold costs the world a tree, and if he wants more books his mother won't be at school picking him up but working full time so as to afford them and not around to read them, choose them or share in them with him. There ended the lesson, but I hated having to get on my high horse over a £4 book.

It spurred me to consider more ways of refocusing children away from consumption to putting in and giving back. Not because they need to be always acting with a view to charity or good deeds, but if nothing else, in order to raise their awareness and challenge their own thinking about the community to which they belong. We should create a movement for change and good in the wider community; find causes and raise the profile of issues. At the very immediate level I applaud the recycle and swap shop themes that are increasingly prevalent these days. Beyond that – for children – it would be so easy and stimulating to have them bring along old books, clothes, toys, boxes, cartons and plastic and use those items to build or create something new. The product of their labour could be displayed and prizes awarded for creativity and innovation and usability. In part, installation art in our community, as well as a living, working communal sense of "mend and make-do"!

We could entice local gardens and community organisations to use some of the talents of the wonderful afterschool gardening club to green up the local environs. The cycle club could help distribute food to old or homeless people in the parish – working with local cafés say – to deliver unused stock.

The list goes on. We need to educate children about far more than how to add the cost of that fairy book to that sticker book and pass their SATs. Little by little, we can start a quiet revolution in the minds of the young people.

So, how are the homeless people? You said they provide a great source of distraction to you during mum's illness? Poor chaps.

I had better sign off. Put an end to the worry for a couple of weeks and enjoy Mummy being home next week with you.

Lots of love

Tess

October 15, 2008

Dear Mum,

I have been very light hearted since lunch time when I received Claire's text saying you were likely to be going home and that your leukaemia cells were much reduced. Dare we call it a remission? Well done, you. You must be delighted and relieved and grateful. You can enjoy a little time at home before the next round of chemo. I am sure the whole family is thrilled and heaving a collective sigh of relief.

I knew you would be alright, you are indomitable, despite how awful this past month has been. Our prayers were answered and a reprieve granted...

I have thought of you constantly over the past few days. I was anxious not to call too often – feeling unsure of what to say other than how much I was hoping and praying for a good prognosis – which I know you knew.

Not much news here since my last letter.

I have now completed another painting. Andrew – who is generally amused by, but supportive of my new hobby - told me about the skills of learning to paint. Basically, the idea is that one needs to learn to draw with a pencil before one picks up a brush. That is fine and good. But you don't tell a knitter they need to practice with macramé first, or tell cross stitchers to go back to year 4 and do some crosses on a gingham tablecloth before they get stuck into a pattern from Peter Jones (very expensive). Can't one just do it? It's not rocket science. One takes a brush and some paint and puts the former in the latter and makes marks on another surface. Crikey – boiling an egg is harder than that.

So, I assured Andrew that the joy was in the doing not the learning, and given my current ambitions to feel free and to express myself through colour, as well as the lack of time for courses and classes, I would just fool around for a bit and enjoy myself and see where it takes me. So on his return from Lagos on the weekend, I asked him if he would like me to do a painting for him. He said yes – a still life. Do you see what I mean – he is amused and indulgent but always a little bit challenging and competitive. Not in a derisory or a malicious way, but in a sort of "I told you so" way.

So, never one to shirk a challenge, I set to work and completed a lovely study of a vase. It is a very close up study of a small bit of one side of the vase, in hues of dark teal green, sage, violet and indigo. He loves it! He conceded that Jackson Pollock had no traditional training.

I am planning to do some green leaves in a blue sky next. I was writing to Claire about some ambition I have for a large modern art installation inspired by our school day breakfast and tooth brushing regimen.

I was telling Marta about my newfound creative energy. She is so supportive and delighted by such things. I think that is why she is so natural and able with children. She delights in the natural expressions of the human spirit – as do children – unselfconscious and uninhibited and free outpourings of consciousness. If you can get that – really live that way without worrying if you are good enough for this or that - then the potential must be huge for achieving real peace in, and enjoyment of, life.

Anyway, I shall stop rambling now. Rest well, eat well if you can and look forward to your going home for a bit.

All my love and overjoyed relief.

Tx

18 October, 2008

Dear Mum,

Had a good day at work today. Learnt a few interesting facts.

1. The department has formed an inclusive senior women's network which welcomes male members.
2. The department has an asexual society – cannot access the members list though – so I might have to join.
3. Music is not allowed in the office building.
4. Many people suffer from a condition which is the opposite of attention deficit disorder (ADD) – ATDD – attention to detail disorder.

ATDD needs to be officially recognised so that research might be funded. There are a huge number of lawyers who have it. There should be support groups for friends and family and co-workers. Sufferers of the disorder would benefit from workshops to help them to spot the difference between actual and rhetorical questions and identify situations in which they should stop speaking (even before finishing their point) because their audience has changed the topic or figuratively or literally moved on. They could also learn ways to stop themselves from citing esoteric points of law or referring to the number of times they have used an unused work of reference or out of print publication. Perhaps it would be better known as BLS (boring lawyer syndrome) for which there really is no help.

This got me thinking about other syndromes I am familiar with through my years in the work force, in particular as a lawyer.

Many young men suffer from TUC: Talk-it-up Complex. Symptoms include gross exaggeration of physical and mental prowess, length of working hours, extent of their influence in and around the office and their capacity for alcohol consumption. More senior professionals will present with oral fixations on their cars, holiday destinations, golf clubs, wine knowledge and success with women. The syndrome is also known as egomania, and in some sufferers, small man syndrome. It should not be confused with the similar but largely psychosomatic condition known as BSS, or Bull Shit Syndrome. This occurs where not even a small morsel of truth lies within the larger story or hyperbole. It is more serious, but as its sufferers tend to be maligned and excluded, those who have the malady rarely rise to the top of the proverbial heap to exert influence or ultimately do too much damage to innocents.

Among women there are three well known personality styles/disorders that have been identified – all three aimed at preventing men from feeling threatened by success or seniority of the said woman. First, we have the Mother complex. Look for bossy speech patterns, sometimes – not always – frumpy apparel, strictness concerning rules and punctuality, praise and incentive focussed performance management tools. The second style is the Seductress/Vixen – say no more – we all know this one, prevalent in all walks of life. Finally, there is the lesser known character, the Psuedo Man. This one can knock back more lagers, tell more ribald jokes and recount more war/rugby stories than the best of the men. Locker rooms are her preferred haunt, she smokes and swears like a trooper and strip clubs name drinks after her.

The rest of the women, myself included, occupy some no-man's land where anything goes, but often the Librarians or the Little Sister or the Work Experience Girl proliferate in the vain attempt to be unthreatening and not manifest too much intelligence, personality or humour. The ploy of these personae is to safeguard their role quietly and often demurely without drawing attention to the fact that they have gained acceptance and even recognition, for their professional and intellectual contributions.

These are mild disorders or syndromes. While they are common they are by no means universal traits. Moreover, I cannot comment with authority about other professions or milieus. I have heard that in some, men and women behave quite differently, even normally.

Meanwhile, outside the workplace, there is a virtual epidemic of PMS: Poor Me Syndrome. Symptoms include laborious detail concerning maladies, complaints about many and varied inconveniences, and sense that one is hard done by or victimised. In men you will often see it when they are recounting stories of lost love, low bonuses, defeat in football matches or suffering with a slight cold. In women the topics can be far more varied. If you are not on the ball you can mistake a PMS sufferer for a new mother having a gripe at a sense of lost identity and independence. But the Prada shoes and the Gucci glasses and the Burberrys coat can be deceiving. A good rule of thumb is to count the number of times the words "I would do/say such and such, but my husband..." are used.

Another giveaway is the frequent reference to themselves as suffering in the face of what might be regarded as superb opportunities. E.g. "Woe is me. I am so tired after spending the weekend away with girlfriends at the Four Seasons. The kids are so rotten and cranky. My life is so hard. My husband does nothing to help. My cleaner is crap. My au pair forgot to take the children to ballet yesterday and now I have to get ready to go to the Opera and all my dresses are at the cleaners. Unbelievable." This is not to be confused with self-absorption which can occasionally manifest in this way. In the later case, the symptoms are far less acute and the speaker is capable of more than a cursory interest in others.

But, you'll know when you come across a PMS sufferer as they are well into their latest whine or complaint while you are still smiling out a forced hello. Sometimes you won't spot them because they can be quite witty and entertaining in many ways. They may have a veneer of pleasant and sunny sociability but lying beneath is a morass of seething discontent. Their venting is really a call for attention and solace and empathy from innocent bystanders, who may not have learnt to recognise the syndrome, or who may be too diplomatic to know how and when to beat the retreat to get home for the plumber or the weather report. I assure you I am not revealing a jealous and uncaring side. I concede that I may be rejecting my shadow; maybe I resent these traits because I cannot own them in myself. Hopefully, recognising this possibility will keep the syndrome at bay.

While the PMS sufferer is essentially harmless; they are their own worst enemy. But they can do damage to the less vigilant. They sap energy and can drain the unwary listeners of the will to live. For this I think that some of the worn down friends or acquaintances might benefit from some sort of humour therapy or even scream workshops. I want to investigate ways of setting up soft walled, soundproofed rooms where the needy could effectively "work out" the tension and release the valve on the accumulating pressure by screaming in a safe and non-judgemental place.

I had a pleasant walk home from school with Jack today after our respective after school activities ended. He remarked: "When something bad happens at school, Pauline sometimes speaks to Jean in French and they discuss it frenchily".

Apparently the French children have been known to exchange glances and converse in this way near or with Jack, to his interest and delight. I am quite clear about what he means and I have adopted the expression whole heartedly. It only works with a few languages and nationalities, though, I caution. It describes the whole arena of verbal and non-verbal communication. While one would love to speak of the Italians and Spanish in a similar way – there is nothing quite like being looked at "frenchily".

Jack also has a word for the way Americans speak – we fondly call this "washing", as we were in Washington D.C. when the phrase was first coined. It is most apt to describe the way they throw in the extra "noise". Y'know what I mean?

With Australians the children seem to be pretty clued in as to the unspoken and less spoken nuances of meaning and intonation as well. I asked Felix who the supply teacher was for his class today and he replied that she was Australian because she said "mate".

Tx

17 October, 2008

Dear Mum

While we only spoke for a moment this morning you sounded very chipper and it was wonderful to hear you laugh! I insist that everything in my letter from the other week is true and you are and did all those wonderful things I wrote about – and millions more.

I had a very pleasant time today as I spent almost three hours dealing with school politics at a parents association meeting and then chatting with a couple of mothers afterwards. No risk of group think or a herd mentality at these get togethers. There must be a different view expressed by most of the parents present about most of the issues. Only after everyone has said their piece do we feel we can move on. It was very interesting to hear the different views. A small proportion of the assembled felt most strongly about the school dinners. A vexing topic at the best of times. Yet in the face of huge overhaul and a revamp of the catering, the menu and the health giving features of the lunches, some mothers still feel that it is not good enough.

I was unsure what to do – whether to interject to move things along. I stood poised physically and metaphorically, to say something reasonable – I could not get a word in. I was struck, after the days earlier this week worrying about your biopsy results, at how our problems are all relative and how really big ones help put the littler ones into perspective. Then again, perhaps my diffidence about the dinners is further confirmation that I am at heart, an average, or even bad, parent. I am not zealous about their diets like those mothers. I give them crisps and sweets for no reason occasionally – well actually, I usually have an excellent reason related to my getting something I want done, distracting them (immunisations for trip to Africa) or buying me some peace. While I am tempted to table some motions for the next meeting, to nip this personal barrow pushing in the bud, I am concerned that I will only alienate the milder elements. I will bide my time and work the back rooms awhile.

Mind you I am not very talented at the politicking. It was an area of my professional development that was somewhat retarded, along with my failure to master the delivery of the sexist jokes around the water cooler.

The corridors of Whitehall have nothing on the aisles of Sainsbury's, the grubby nooks in Starbucks or the rustic communal table at the more chi-chi Pain Quotidian, not to mention the line at the school gate at 3.30pm. I think much extreme child oriented power broking also takes place on weekends, after swimming or football, when children are released and playing freely or at the birthday parties or play dates, where the adults can orchestrate their little manoeuvres and push their barrows. I think some of the husbands are very smooth operators as well. I imagine things also occur of a Saturday evening in the conservatories and reception rooms over rosé and crème brulée, but I don't get out to know about that first hand.

I suppose the political campaigns for popularity, information and influence are merely preparation for life. But while millions of children go to bed hungry with no parent to care for them, let alone cook a nutritious meal with all the food groups represented, we sit there, over our skinny soy lattes, frustrated that our children might have imbibed less than an ideal calorie.

If I could just coach myself into having enough backbone to interject in the meetings or around the coffee cups, then I might not need this outlet here...

I should go. *NCIS* is about to start. It's the one where Tony gets the plague!

Much love

Tx

17 October, 2008

Dear Mum,

I am back and I have come up with a sure fire solution to my aforementioned issues about lack of, or rather, differences in, parenting perspective.

Yes; a quiz. This quiz could be given out to all new parents on enrolling their child at school. It would provide useful, even invaluable, insight to the school governors, head teacher and the parents association as to just what they are in for in a given year. Forewarned is forearmed. Now, if we consider primary school, the real value would lie in the participants being self-aware enough to be able to answer a range of questions which might yet be only hypothetical, as their children would be young, and in some regards the ground would be untested. More relevant to secondary transfers perhaps? However, like my Lovelorn questionnaire, an eye-opening quiz could assist all parents recognize their styles and those of others, and gain appreciation and tolerance of one another's perspectives. I have written two quizzes below. The first, since we were on the topic already, is focussed on parenting of school age children, say pre-teens. The second is geared at relatively new parents, blissfully unaware of the minefield ahead of them.

Let me know what you think.

School Parenting Style Questionnaire

1. How did you select the school your child attends?

a) Location and recommendations.
b) Quality of teaching, leaderships and test results.
c) Cost.
d) Attitude to discipline.
e) Alumni connections.

2. Of the following potential problems at school for your child, which would present the greatest challenge to you as a parent?

a) Nits and worms, diet and illness, if he or she was not clever.
b) Poor teaching quality or favouritism.
c) Forking out for extras.
d) Bullying.
e) Poor socialisation.

3. So far, what has pleased or excited you most about your child's school life?

a) Preparing for tests.
b) Seeing my child make friends and get excited about the work.
c) The class trip to the stock exchange.
d) The crackdown on bullying.
e) His/her star role in all the plays.

4. How do you reward your child for good work at school?

a) Shopping trips, staying up late, new toys.
b) With praise, a cuddle, a sticker.
c) Money.
d) Are you kidding?
e) Play dates.

5. If you could change anything at the school what would it be?

a) The toilet facilities, the meals, the curriculum, the play equipment, my level of access.
b) The mind sets.
c) The fees.
d) The political correctness.
e) The amount of homework.

6. What is your best memory of your primary school days?

a) The exams.
b) So many – learning, friends, games.
c) Pocket money.
d) Leaving.
e) Parties.

7. If you could give your child one piece of advice for his or her school days, what would it be?

a) Winning isn't everything, it's the only thing.
b) Work hard, try hard, have fun.
c) You don't have to share or get along with everyone.
d) Never go the bathroom alone.
e) Always strive to be the teacher's "pet".

8. What do you hope for your child?

a) Academic success, status and slimness.
b) Happiness and fulfilment of potential.
c) A well paid job.
d) To come out alive.
e) To be popular.

9. Which extra-curricular activities would you encourage your children to take up?

a) Basketball, football, judo.
b) Cricket, debating, art.
c) None.
d) Chess, computers.
e) Ballet, drama, cooking.

10. What is best thing about your child's school?

a) Parents like me.
b) The community as a whole.
c) Its free.
d) High value placed on discipline.
e) My social network.

For parents of younger children:

Parenting Style Questionnaire

1. What is the single biggest challenge you have faced to date as a parent?

a) Potty training.
b) Child care.
c) Financial pressure.
d) Behaviour.
e) Mother-in-law's interference.

2. What do you love most about being a parent?

a) Achieving milestones.
b) Seeing the world through my child's eyes.
c) I have a great excuse to stay home and not spend money.
d) Having a little friend.
e) Dressing my child up.

3. What do you dislike most about being a parent?

a) Occasional loss of control.
b) Curbs on my freedom of movement.
c) Financial pressure.
d) Tantrums.
e) Stretch marks.

4. How do you resolve conflicts over parenting issues with your partner?

a) There is no conflict – I tell him what we will be doing.
b) Discussion, taking advice from others.
c) We agree on most things that matter and I keep my mouth shut on everything else.
d) Haranguing can be effective.
e) Rely on my mother, his mother or the nanny to sort it.

5. What annoys you most about other parents?

a) That they do things differently from me.
b) It varies, but smoking springs to mind.
c) Lax financial management.
d) Indulging bad behaviour.
e) Whinging.

ZOË COPLEY

6. What do you wish you had known before you became a parent?

a) How hard it can be to be the best at everything.
b) How hard it is to leave them with strangers.
c) How much they cost me.
d) How to stop them from crying.
e) How to not gain extra weight during pregnancy.

7. What, if anything, do you regret about parenting so far?

a) Choice of father.
b) Worrying over the right work/life balance.
c) Not having more money in the bank.
d) Sparing the rod.
e) It's all great really.

8. What is your idea of an ideal parent?

a) A slim, well-dressed confident woman with good looking, intelligent prize winning children.
b) Someone who imbues confidence and thoughtfulness in their children.
c) Someone who teaches their child right from wrong.
d) A model of good manners and calmness.
e) Someone who looks after themselves; if the mother is happy...

9. What are you most looking forward to as a parent?

a) The graduation days.
b) Everything really.
c) Knowing they will take care of me in old age.
d) Their adulthood.

e)   The shopping.

10. What advice would you give to someone soon to become a parent for the first time?

a)   The sleep deprivation is a killer – make sure your partner pulls his weight.
b)   Enjoy it – it goes fast.
c)   Look after your finances – they'll bleed you dry.
d)   Scotch guard everything and don't get carried away – one is enough.
e)   Never scrimp on good help.

The analysis of the results will go as follows:

Results:

If you answered mostly As then you have an Ambitious and High Achieving parenting style. You call a spade a spade and do not suffer fools gladly. You want the best for your child and will push to make sure he or she gets it. You believe that no one knows more than you about most things. This means that you tend to be zealous in expressing your viewpoint and unforgiving of other or divergent experiences. You value academic excellence and trappings of status highly. You will typically set extra homework for your child, enrol him or her in several extra activities and expect top results in all pursuits. You run the risk of burning your child out at a young age.

If you answered mostly Bs then you seem to approach parenting in an open and receptive way. While you value excellence and rigour you will not expect more than your child can deliver. You parent with an eye to having fun and inspiring confidence and try to be fair in you treatment of your children. While not a perfectionist you do set high standards. You run the risk of being sentimental about childhood.

If you answered mostly Cs then your main concerns are financial. You are focussed on providing well for your child, without overextending your finances or taking on undue risk. You value conservative and common sense approaches to parenting and problem solving. You will instil similar values in your child and will teach them frugality, prudence and the value of planning. You are not distracted by frivolity. Rather, you imbue a sense of responsibility in your child. Your run the risk of raising tight arses.

If you answered mostly Ds then your main concern is for your child to not be too traumatised by its childhood experiences, probably because your own loom large in your memory. You are mindful of issues of safety and security, good behaviour and strong discipline. Your way is "old-school", with emphasis on fitting in and not attracting attention to your child, especially where bullying or socialisation is concerned. You run the risk of over protecting your child from all of life's adventures and creating a bore.

If you answered mostly Es then your main concern is yourself. You enjoy your children. You delegate the tedious, difficult or serious elements of parenting. You value fun, popularity and style over academic pursuits or discipline. You manage stress well; you are happy and relaxed with parenthood. You run the risk of raising an airhead.

Thought provoking? I know there are many more personality foibles and styles of parenting, but do you think I have the main bases covered here? I cover my backside by stating this is a tool. As such it is not right, nor the only tool, but like all tools, it is useful.

Speak soon.

With love

Tx

19 October, 2008

Dear Mum,

You sounded well today when we spoke. Strong and bright and energetic.

We ended up not taking the "crunchy" train today. We stayed in town and had a quiet afternoon. Andrew returns from Washington tomorrow, so we are looking forward to a Sunday together. Hopefully we will achieve more than the standard big shop at Sainsbury's. It is hard to get more done when he is jetlagged, but equally, the grocery shopping could keep til he leaves again. I think he likes doing the shopping; he rarely steps foot in a store in Nigeria. Maybe it's a domestic ritual that helps him feel connected to his family life.

Speaking of connection to family life, I was shopping in Waitrose the other day and I was in the toiletries aisle. In this particular Waitrose the soaps and toothpaste are located opposite the feminine hygiene products, medicines and nappies. I was looking for an anti-bacterial hand soap when a couple passed by across the aisle from where I stood. She was quite attractive, probably mid to late thirties; he was tall and conservatively dressed in brown "slacks", a checked shirt and a brown windbreaker style jacket, balding head. Not horrible, but not handsome either. As they passed me his hand was behind her, resting on her lower back, the other hand carrying a basket and he said – "Do we need anything here? Pads?" I was horrified. First, what sort of man shops for sanitary pads? Second, what sort of man refers to them in public? Third, what sort of man knows where they are located, what they are and initiates a discussion concerning whether they are needed? Finally, who would refer to the decision to purchase them in the plural, "we"?

Perhaps yet again, this is proof of what an anachronistic existence I lead. I am the only person in the locker room who is not striding around in the buff. I think that feminine hygiene products are the reserve of women, to be purchased if not in secret, at least in a discreet and semi-private way, much as one would purchase over the counter medicine for a rather embarrassing complaint. I did not think I was particularly up tight on the whole, though certainly on the modest side of the fence in regards to most of these sorts of things. However, I am beginning to see that there are swathes of society who live in a very open and laissez-faire fashion. Perhaps Andrew too, would love to fill the basket with the unmentionable ladies items, but is too fearful of my Victorian prudery to dare.

Hell, I have had three children. I am no stranger to normal human experience and processes, but by the same token, I maintain that some things are just not for public consumption. The idea that we all want to see other people's naked bodies is rather presumptuous. It's bad enough having to see the tops of their (as Jack would call them) knickers constantly displayed beneath, or rather above, low riding trousers, but this gym striptease etiquette and the idea that the men are out shopping for tampons leaves me wondering just where one can go for a little privacy and respect.

Sometimes I wonder if the over 60s and I are the only women shopping for full brief undies these days. It's a huge responsibility to feel that I alone have to keep the cotton growers in business and the racks at Marks & Spencer stocked with normal briefs. And while I have discreetly raised this at the school gate and found some sympathisers who prefer a brief on the grounds of comfort, I still don't think the numbers of us resisting the other varieties of underwear can be large enough to sustain a market.

I know that I sound like a "grumpy old woman" and that most

people would advise me to chill out and relax. We are all human and we all have bodies and they are beautiful and to be prized etc etc etc. If that were true, we would all still be in the Garden (of Eden) naked all the time. We don't regard our bowel function as acceptable public conversation starters do we? Have I missed the modern trend on that one too?

Perhaps I have some sort of deep seated fear of intimacy with my fellow man/woman. Maybe I am a cold fish, shying away from unifying forms of contact. It's true that I shy from many forms of contact. And yet I hold doors for people and stand back to let others queue before me. The gym is the best microcosm in which to assess one's appetite for intimacy. In the UK there is a tendency to stand close to other people generally. Probably due to the denser living conditions and the cold weather. But at the gym, I do find it rather off-putting.

Consider this, for example. I am at the gym. I have laid out a mat, my towel a couple of hand weights and a ball – 65cm diameter, soft, inflated rubber thing that one uses to aid the exercise regimen. I am in the middle of a self-styled circuit using the aforementioned equipment and some weight machines located right by my mat. Along comes another gym member who takes the ball, moves the mat and then plonks her own stuff right next to mine – literally 20 centimetres from my book. Oh, and the entire area - approximately 16 square metres of floor space - is otherwise unoccupied. It boggles the mind just what was going on there. So I return to my mat. I don't move it back to the original position, but leave it where it was shoved. I take another ball from the ball stand and glance at the protagonist. She is oblivious to my existence – she is tuned into her iPod stretching away with my ball, engrossed in her abdominal muscles, blissfully unaware of her, in gym speak, trespass. I would think that the sweaty towel on the mat would be a giveaway that the mat and equipment were still in use (not to mention the half empty water bottle, mobile phone and book), but at no point did it occur to her that eye contact, a smile, a shrug of acknowledgment of any form was warranted. Either she is one rude gym bunny or just plain stupid.

Perhaps the problem lies with me. Maybe I am invisible. I should get coaching to improve my presence and increase my personal impact. Even so, it was all too close for comfort. Why do people want to be right next to a stranger when there is loads of free space? But it's the same on the tube – if you had a choice of seat wouldn't you favour a spot with no one either side of you?

Maybe the pressure of exercising brings out the meanness in us all. One day I spotted a fat and flabby guy sweating away as he hoisted the 5 kg dumbbells. He was alternating use of these with some weight machines nearby - as one does - and I noticed his routine involved at least a five minute interval where the 5's were not in use.

So I smiled and asked if I could borrow the 5's for a minute, saying I would give them back as soon as he needed them. The sighing and eye rolling that then ensued would have astounded anyone. The graceless, discourteous reluctance to share was infantile at best. Now, I know, when people do those big exhalations and dramatic hand gestures they are passively aggressively showing you they cannot bear the idea of what you suggested and are effectively refusing to acquiesce, provided you are thoroughly embarrassed and mollified following their display of being put out. You are supposed to slink away mortified by the boldness of your suggestion. This theatrical act of being so terribly put upon was of no effect, though, on me. I decided that not only was he deserving of inconvenience, imagined, rather than real, but his reaction belied such an egotistical and foul personality that I was determined to match it. Rather than quietly move away – what most people would do on realising they were dealing with a psychopath - I decided (fired up about gym sharing issues as a general rule, you see) to give my best back – so I said in my most sarcastic tones: "hey sorry, don't worry! I can wait til you are done. I would hate to interrupt the flow here".

Well, at that, he strode off, muttering expletives under his breath and fetched himself another set of 5's from the far end of the room. I called after him in my sweetest voice: "Hey sorry, let me get those", thereby suggesting to any onlookers that the fat boy couldn't carry his own weights. I did not see him again for months. Then suddenly I realised he had moved to another part of the gym. He was virtually unrecognisable. He is slim, toned and wears body builders gloves and gut belt. Did I contribute to this metamorphosis? Was he so ashamed that he was only lifting 5 kilo dumbbells that he transformed himself?

It seems that stamina and fitness is just as competitive an arena as long working hours. I used to swim laps of the pool until I realised that the whole process was too tiring.

First, without prescription goggles or contact lenses I struggle to see the end, the ropes and the other swimmers. Secondly, there is not enough room, especially when the men swimmers decide it is time for a little bit of butterfly to finish off their workout. Third, sharing a lane with a man is so endlessly strategic and exhausting as to take all the fun out of swimming. The great thing about laps is that one ought to be able to switch off and freely think one's thoughts as one exercises. But this "lap dance" with the men is all about seeming to be faster or to be in front. Now I stay well away from the lap swimmers and just paddle about in the recreation lanes. They may think I am a freak, especially as I bob and bounce with spectacles on, but thankfully no one wants to compete with that. Thankfully, also, the pool at my gym has a large proportion of foreign - i.e. non–British - users, so the overall standard of swimming ability is good. When I first came to London the users of the Queen Mother Sports Centre at Victoria were terrible swimmers. Uncoordinated and flabby and slow and yet convinced by the fact they were in the water that they were the next Ian Thorpe. After a couple of months of horrible and virulent colds and flu it dawned on me that, while the non-British swimmers could in fact swim well, their persistent spitting of steaming phlegm globules into the water was going to kill me in the end.

No doubt such images are not uncommon on the cancer ward so I will finish here.

Lots of love.

Tx

21 October, 2008

Dear Mum,

Lovely to hear that you spoke with Andrew today and that you had some time out of hospital and expect to head home tomorrow or the next day. Did it feel like day release from prison? (How would you know?) Was the sky a weird shade of blue and the bird song deafening, after weeks on the ward?

I am looking forward to speaking to you once you are safely ensconced in your own home. Sorry I have not called for a couple of days. It has been very busy of a morning and I tried today before we left for school but the phone would not connect to your room. You must have been out!

We are all well. Today was a glorious autumn day. Vivid sky of deep blue and leaves turning bright orange. It felt like the air was washed clean after an evening of rain last night.

I am trying to refocus on my coaching and my after school club now after a few weeks of distraction. I am going to finalise my website and some flyers and try to generate some interest around the local community for group coaching and homework and communication support for children. If I can manage to fit things into the time that the boys are already with Marta then I will not be compromising with my own children in the process.

Work is fine. I am looking forward to Thursday back in the office as we always have our team meeting and there is usually some interesting learning to be had. I was reviewing a recent High Court judgment and came across a wonderfully expressed description of what is essentially my day-to-day working role. I have extracted it for your enlightenment. Mr Justice Norris said:

> *"It is something of a disgrace that in order to work out the tax consequences of an entirely ordinary commercial transaction one must refer to about 20 closely articulated and specific statutory provisions replete with cross references: and it is a matter of no great credit that the eventual method of charging tax is to postulate a notional sum paid under a hypothetical obligation, which notional payment is then itself treated "as if" it was something else so that it can be deemed to affect the repurchase price and create a fictional income flow. Having entered into such a maze of hypothesis, notion, fiction and deeming it would be no surprise to discover that the draftsman did not find himself quite where he intended or facing the direction he thought[5]."*

Considering I have worked both on structuring and finessing the so-called commercial transactions, as well as drafting the underlying legislative provisions, I felt that he was almost speaking directly to me. There was a great sense of connection and empathy, not something I have heretofore really had, in my dealings with the judiciary. The very idea that one can be required to interpret the law and that the law can be described in terms of hypothetical, notional, deeming and fictional is so ridiculous as to be almost unbelievable. I think it is just this sort of thing that renders me incapable of normal curiosity and surprise at myriad sensationalist headlines.

I have been considering the pricing of my coaching services and trying to benchmark their value against other commodities available in the market. As I am a little out of touch with products not available in Waitrose, Boots, Waterstones or cafés, it has been fascinating to discover the price the market will bear for entertainment and services. For example, in my neighbourhood,

---

5 DCC Holdings (UK) Ltd v HM Revenue & Customs [2008] EWHC 2429 (Ch) (17 October 2008) at para 22.

swimming lessons cost over £25 pounds per half hour, decent seats at the theatre are now over £40 pounds, concert tickets are off the charts, massages are at least £60 pounds per hour, individual pilates classes are the same price. Haircuts vary as you would know, but one tends to get what one pays for. While my oriental health clinic offers incredible value reflexology and massages, it is truly aberrant that it is pricing these services so competitively, and they are fabulous as well. The girls work really hard, dripping with perspiration during the deep tissue massage, the sweat included in the price. They are incredibly strong and I always come out of the treatment in agony. No pain, no gain.

So what is the value of an hour of my coaching – sweat included but agony optional? How long is a piece of string?

I will sign off now – need to have something to eat and get back to my novel.

Tx

22 October 2008

Dear Mummy,

What a delight to have you calling me today letting me know you are home. We are all so pleased that you are feeling well and are back where you belong. Do take it easy though. It must be lovely to be free of the drugs and the drip, the infections and discomfort and even the nurses and doctors, and to have some sort of normalcy back.

Now that you are home again I will probably lose the motivation to write to you. Though I have enjoyed the opportunity to put so much down on paper. I will perhaps keep up the writing so as to not tire you out with long phone conversations just yet.

What is news here? I had a productive and busy day today with Tommy. I am testing the waters regarding running group coaching workshops for women and so I had a very useful chat at playgroup. While I would not target mothers only, it was a useful starting point to gauge interest levels and appetite for the workshop style approach as well as helping me to determine a price for the service.

I was very energised by the idea that my small coaching practice could become a business reality and that I could be instrumental in facilitating transformations like that which I experienced over the spring and summer. I was, I have to admit, beginning to lose heart over the past couple of weeks. I had started to convince myself that it was all a bit "out there", especially during difficult financial times. Who wants to bellyache about themselves and pay for the privilege? Then I had a great coaching session on Monday which put it all into perspective. My coach, Jennifer, from my course, suggested that I could let myself off the hook for dropping the coaching ball over the past few weeks given that since returning from Australia 7 weeks ago my mind has been diverted to wondering what would be happening with you. That recognition and acceptance was very liberating and a massive floodgate has lifted.

There is so much bursting through it that I am carrying a notebook around with me to record my ideas in as I have them, for fear of losing them. I am having original thoughts as well as refining kernels of ideas that have been swimming round in my mind for months, looking for a place to find fertile ground.

Anyway, it is all very positive. I plan to gather a small group of women together for an introductory session at home and demonstrate what coaching is and how it can work. I will convince some of them to sign up for workshops as well as generate some word of mouth interest. I am also formulating the next steps for the children's coaching offering and how to provide parents with some coaching support directly in relation to children's communication and learning issues as they arise at home.

I will send you my promotional material to peruse when it is ready!

I am enjoying work a lot more now as well and have initiated a dialogue with HR to see if I can offer coaching services in–house. So far the response is positive. Perhaps my plan to be coaching full time by next September is not so unfeasible after all.

On that happy note I will go now and edit my little draft advertisement.

Lots of love to Dad and Claire and the boys.

Tx

24 October 2008

Dear Mum,

You sounded very strong and back to normal on the phone this morning. I am thrilled to hear you speaking so positively and enthusiastically about just being home. Fingers crossed that all the leukaemia is gone for good. I hope you have a lovely visit with Janet next week. Send my best to Rob and wish him well with the business. He is definitely not embarking on a coaching career, and is training as a hairdresser instead? Maybe I will run workshops for self employed men. There is no reason to restrict myself to women – other than the fact that men are more openly competitive, less forthcoming about personal issues in groups, tend to go on too long about themselves if they do get started and less available during the day....

Maybe I will pilot a programme at work for the lawyer men. We could do all sorts of things. "Coaching for performance – the secrets of style", "Dress for success in the civil service", or "What not to say and when not to say it – a workshop on humour and pathos in the workplace".

We could also do a lot with jargon and avoiding acronyms – across the board really.

I was thinking about all the terms that are my stock in trade as a lawyer and how they have no meaning in any other milleu. Of course some have become common parlance; the law permeates everyday society and conversation, but equally there are many that have no real meaning.

I have a session with my children at the afterschool club based on developing dictionary skills where we try to guess what unfamiliar words mean and create alternative meanings. In that vein, for my own amusement, I prepared a list of legal, tax and accounting terms and their meanings with an audience of "normal" people in mind.

Here is a sample:

- Closely held company – someone you like to hug.
- Holding company – the friend who minds your bag when you're in the toilet.
- Group relief – the after effects of venting in a small group coaching workshop, also a term for the collective button/fly loosening that occurs after a very big lunch.
- Substance over form – when the kids spill your wine/Bolognese on the tax return.
- Stamp duty – the chore of queuing in the post office.
- Consideration – what the mother gets too little of.
- Liquidation – ignoring the use by date and pouring the milk in the tea and cereal and hoping no one notices (liquid-day-shun).
- Garnishment – the art of elaborately decorating the dinner/serving plate.
- Succession – being oblivious to or unimpressed by winning (success – shun).
- Bad debt – a bill for a garment you've never worn.
- Title report – what you have when the book club don't bother reading the book.
- Hegde funds – the neighbours' reluctant cash contribution to greening up the common wall.
- Self assessment – how you feel about yourself.
- Accrual basis – unkind way of treating someone.
- Adjusting entry – standing back to let someone else in first.
- Allocate - a greeting to Catherine.
- Amortise – a dead and lifeless gaze (mine after too long with an ATDD sufferer).

- Carrying cost – money spent on treating post pregnancy backache.
- Convertible bond – the camaraderie between sports car owners.
- Copyright – acceptable or effective imitation of the cool kids.
- Fringe benefits – the youth giving impact of covering forehead wrinkles.
- First in first out – a rule that never applies at the 10am family mass.
- Libor – the person who tediously talks themselves and their experiences up.
- Par value of preferred stock – the cost of being the favourite child.
- Weighted average – your median weight across the festive season.
- Hurdle rate – the number of barriers your child can scale at sports day compared to his class mates.
- Manufactured interest – feigned delight with conversation at school gate.
- Loan maturity – what small children tend to be (low-on).
- Novation – staying at home for half term (no- va(ca)tion).
- Transitional provisions – arrangements made for hand over by old nanny to new.

And some coaching euphemisms translated:

- Did that land? – Is my new age self help lingo making sense yet?
- How do you want me to be? – Which annoying parts of my personality are going to drive you mental over the next hour?
- What does that look like? – Whose life are you hoping to copy in order to achieve that future?
- How will we know when we are there? – What is your budget for these sessions?

I think that it also applies with educators too:

- Socialisation – how your kid bullies or is bullied.
- Strong personality – bloody little pain in the neck that no one likes.
- Meeting targets – a useful one as it can mean any of – annoyingly clever and challenging, boringly average or have no idea because targets are ridiculous and meaningless.

Hope you are still feeling strong and cheerful by the time I have done my stamp duty and this reaches you next week.

Lots of love,

Tx

26 October, 2008

Dear Mum,

The clocks went back to winter time today. While most people look forward to the last Saturday in October for the extra hour of sleep it brings them, I dread it. The dark nights descend gloomily, the children wake at 5.30am (on a Sunday) and the drizzly Autumn weather that one was trying to see as novel and exciting suddenly becomes depressing and grim.

We made the most of the day, nevertheless, by swimming, going to mass and having lunch out with Kate. The boys always love seeing her and being the only cousin here it is very lovely to spend time with her. I was running some of my group coaching ideas past her and she suggested I run "getting away from it" weekends for women. Imagine, a way to have a tax deductible spa break with no children. No wonder she is in PR.

She is also a great sounding board for me when considering the singles and 20-something market for coaching – if there is one. I subconsciously associate it with older people or niche coaching for children, and risk missing a whole target audience. The young, hip, alive people who are happily bouncing from job to job and relationship to relationship, blissfully unaware of crow's feet, sleep deprivation, ominous decisions, seem to be outside my reach. And yet, that must trivialise the experiences of a large potential market. But as I have said before, the philosophical underpinning of coaching is that anyone can benefit from having a place to think and plan and an objective and supportive listener to help channel that process. I will just have to become a little more cyber aware and hip, in order to access the Gen Y client base.

I have been considering the way that TV shows portray certain types of people. In particular, all the drama series that rely on stereotypes and melodrama to hook the viewer. And yet, when you consider the success of *Cath and Kim*, there is proof that the mundane and the vulgar is truly bewitching material. We revel in the schadenfreude of believing we are better or cleverer than the protagonists. It's the opposite of *Friends* and *Will and Grace* and the like where we, the audience, *wanted* their lives and their hair and their apartments.

I want to create a sitcom for the credit crunch. A facetious look at life in the semi-detached houses of west London during the late noughties as the well-to-do face a coming down to earth. Even if the current financial strain doesn't in fact last very long, there would still be a series or two's mileage to be had from a portrayal of Kensington's desperate housewives. Why is there no realistic portrayal of that sort of person's existence? We have programmes doing the working class scene and various dramatisations of the legal genre, the criminal, the medical and the upper class. But few come to mind that provide a view of the silent majority. And the offerings from America that purport to do this; *Desperate Housewives*, *The OC* or *Big Love*, even *Six Feet Under*, rely either on completely suspended reality and glamour or quirky niche subjects like polygamy and undertaking to hook us in.

My idea is that the viewer be introduced to five women and given a snapshot of their lives as at 2009-10. Not exciting stuff, but humorous and real. Maybe a "No Sex and the Suburbs". The power of the series would lie in its universal reach, the fact that the audience would feel like they knew the characters and their lives, indeed *were* the characters. It would rely on biting and slick humour to spice up the otherwise ordinary storylines of the characters day-to-day existences. Sort of condensing a year's drama into a couple of episodes. I want to bring out the humanity and generousness of them; the often complex and conflicting yearnings and dreams of the characters. The fact is, that middle age spread, holidays at home and giving up the Saturday night babysitter are a big deal for lots of people.

The show would be based around a core group of five women who somewhat surprisingly are good friends – having met and stayed in touch following ante-natal classes in 2000. The poetic licence – or maybe it's called dramatic licence - would lie in the fact that in real life such disparate types would have moved or grown apart over 8 years. So for the sake of the dialogue and the set pieces of the show, it will be crucial that these very different women are the centrepiece of the drama.

I will let that stew for a couple of days and tell you more next time I write.

In the meanwhile, how is it, being at home? Are you forever changed by your experiences with leukaemia such that the little things no longer annoy you? Or do they seem even worse? It intrigues me just how you must be managing. Do you feel as if everything is rosy and sparkly and touched by the grace of God?

We had a very lovely sermon at mass today delivered by our resident deacon. It was based on the idea that God's love has no end and that we can and must love ourselves as our neighbour. After all, God loves us with all our faults. It was a half full mass and we were the only young family. Predictably, Tommy saw fit to speak at the top of his voice all through the liturgy of the Eucharist which was very embarrassing. Even after taking him to the back, he shushed me loudly, demanded my lipstick, screamed in anger at Felix who took his coin for the plate and yelled at me: "Mummy be quiet! I am singin' a song." Unlike when we attend the family mass, he was the loudest and worst behaved child there. I was the mortified and incompetent mother struggling to command respect and authority. Thank goodness the sermon had preached love and understanding.

The man at the back who gave me a withering stare as I tried to salvage some dignity and remove Tommy, can contemplate his Christian charity and love over his roast lamb tonight. Indeed it has given me some pause for thought. I am sure God understands. But if we all took that line we would overlook a lot of things wouldn't we? On the one hand, suffer the little children; on the other, shut them the hell up or take them out. By the end of today's service I was a mess, hanging out for a rest and even a glass of wine to take the edge off my tension headache. You see, this sort of challenge would be great fodder for the sitcom.

I should go and catch some *NCIS* before I do a painting. I did a beautiful cloud last night. It was very therapeutic. I might try a leaf tonight or grass – imagine a very close, close up of a small detail of the grass. That is what I aim to capture.

Lots of love.

Tx

30 October, 2008

Dear Mum,

Hope you are still feeling very well and relaxed when you receive this letter. While the schedule of check ups every 48 hours is arduous it must be very reassuring to have positive blood test results each time. I hope it continues into next week and up to the point where they begin the next round of chemo.

I have just painted you a picture. It is an orangey white rendition of some tulips. It's rather lovely, albeit amateurish. The great thing about painting, unlike many other forms of expression, is that it is forgiving. The talentless can still express and enjoy and create something lovely. One can't really say the same about say, cooking, architecture, singing, dancing, tennis, driving...

I had hoped to spend a little time on my screenplay this week, but instead I have been up late working on my coaching marketing material and website design. An awful lot of hours have been spent on that, it must be said. I am using a template provided by the web host but even so, getting the content and pictures just right is quite time consuming (but fun!). I have printed invitations for a coffee morning to launch my group coaching workshops. I am going to tell them what it is all about and offer a free sample session – a taster, for a willing potential client. They will see the power and transformative process at work in my living room. If any of the invitees show up... hopefully a few will come and spread the word amongst their networks and gradually a client base will emerge. I should also do an evening session for working people to come to.

The boys are on half term vacation and they seem to be getting on each other's nerves with alarming frequency. It is stretching my creative reserves and providing me with resources that I can use in coaching. There is no teacher like experience.

We went to the Tate Britain Gallery today. It was a horrible rainy day with a cold wind and cold drenching rain that gets into your shoes and down your back. My hair was plastered to my head as I cannot manage an umbrella with the pushchair. I am trying to get the boys out to the various galleries now that they have the capacity to endure the crowds and wander through for a while. Having said that, it is really me that cannot endure the crowds.

The Tate has a regular Saturday art trolley where children select a tray full of various materials - fabric, paper, string - tape and glue and go off to some corner of the gallery to create something based on one of the exhibitions. For example, one could do a self portrait or a landscape. We picked up our supplies of art material in the shadow of a battle painting by none other than John Singleton Copley. It put my recent foray into painting in the shade.

We chose a place in the main foyer area on the ground floor of the gallery where they often stage short term exhibitions. There we were able to experience a new display themed "speed". Basically, 6 or 7 men dressed in running clothes ran through the central foyer area at full speed every 2 minutes or so. The runners had been told to run flat out, as if for their lives for 30 second bursts. This was designed to create an artistic spectacle. It was illustrative of the lovely wide purview of modern art and the fusion between the living and the static. The whole world is the canvas you see. Well the boys really wanted to join in the canvas, as you can imagine. On a rainy day inside a huge empty space, it was difficult to persuade them these runners were not merely crazy guys come in from the wet and that anyone was free to run too. There was a novelty factor to it – one wondered what it was for - until one read the display explaining "speed". It was clever and fun and memorable and conveyed quite a lot.

It seems though, and this occurred to me a couple of weeks ago, regarding a modern art installation at the Tate Modern, that almost anything could qualify as art. Why not just pour out a huge quantity of cooked spaghetti and throw coloured tins of paint into it, with a chair or two scattered about. Call it "the secret of the universe" or "linguini lingo" or some other obtuse moniker. That's art.

And if I displayed one of my pictures most people would be unimpressed and call it childish and unaccomplished and condemn my effort for want of talent or lack of execution and suggest art classes might help.

Now if I rent some space in Soho or Mayfair and create an exhibition of living three dimensional art themed on life in the slow lane of raising children I could clean up. The gift, the joy, the genius, is in seeing the artistic in the banal; in using everyday objects to evoke meaning and to convey a message. Is that not great art? To connect with many, to strike a chord, to speak to their hearts? And not even resorting to poo, shock, extremism or offense.

I am thinking also of launching the blog after all - in the form of an agony aunt site with letters seeking advice. I would have themed weeks: romance, parenting, job malaise, finding your voice. It could cover the whole gamut of things one could bring to coaching in fact. I would not claim any expertise or superior qualification, just a fresh, ill-informed perspective. But, unlike most advice one receives, the agony aunt is in the truly privileged position of having been asked for an opinion.

A part of me wonders if in fact this is not what coaching really wants to be. I am not sure that all people want to find their own answers after a sometimes confronting search within themselves. I think a lot of people want to be *told* what to do and how to do it.

That is not to say that coaching has no role but if I want to make a living doing this I may need to cover more bases.

I shall speak to you before you receive this – but lots of love.

Tx

2 November 2008

Dear Louise,

Many thanks for the loan of the psychotherapy book enclosed and apologies for keeping it so long. I cannot believe it is almost two months since I saw you in Brisbane. The book was very thought provoking, but I was a little concerned that so many of life's problems seem to be ascribable to a failure to make the appropriate separation from the mother in infancy. I know this is only one thesis of psychotherapy, but it sort of detracts from the whole range of experiences that one has through one's life which form and mould one. So someone fails to make the correct separation and to recognise the father in the family and in the life of the mother? Are they necessarily stuffed thereafter? Does my concern about Mum amount to this very problem? Or have I misunderstood the separation concept?

And what about my children? Andrew is rarely home, so while they associate him with Africa and work and planes and lots of boy things, like tennis and golf, they have very little data that associates their father with their mother. Accordingly, they have never needed to separate from me, except to spend time at school or with a babysitter. So where does that leave them? Are we jeopardising them with this absence thing? Is it too late?

And will the absence be compounded by the other huge errors I have made like returning to work, having them share a room, sending them to a state school, not introducing a second language by now, not forcing Jack into boys' team sports by age 5? Then there are the sweets and the fact that I tell them they cannot have everything they want in life but must choose and maybe even miss out. They will hardly stand a chance against the other children. I am not sure whether the ones who never hear "no" are better prepared for life than the ones who get everything they could imagine ever wanting, before they realise they want or need or like it, but speak so nicely and have such lovely manners.

I guess the world is run by the latter group as adults. And that is why people like you and I are requalifying to follow new careers in our thirties, and still queuing in supermarkets to buy three for two offers on strawberries and perpetuating this myth with our kids, as if it won't feel so bad if we just make sure we surround ourselves with people who think like us.

I apologise for the typing. I have been typing a letter to Mum every few days since we learnt she was ill. It has been a great way to keep in touch, though I have not sent most of the letters. Above all, it lets me feel connected to her and Dad (I seem ok with him and his role in the family, so I am sure that book had nothing to do with me and my neuroses) despite the distance and the fact I don't know when I might be able to visit again. While not a diary – it has served in a way as a therapeutic outlet for some of my thoughts. And so I am in the way of typing a letter at night and out of the way of writing – legibly. So forgive me the formal looking text – I shall find a suitably informal font to put this in before I sign off. Having said that, I had a pen-friend who typed to me once. I stopped corresponding as it seemed just too precious for an 8 year old. Just remember that typing was my worst subject at school – how the mighty are fallen.

Apart from needing to send you the enclosed book, I was thinking of you a lot today as we bought ABBA Gold and the nostalgic reminiscing it evoked had me in mind of you. Tommy was singing "all of us are crying!" at the top of his voice in the bath tonight. I found it rather hard to explain to him what "My Waterloo" really means.

When Jack asked who or what is Fernando I finally realised it is a boy's name. And Chiquiquita? What is that about? It was super to have them all singing and dancing to ABBA thirty years after I first did so. I think it almost equals my delight at their being captivated by the *Sound of Music* last year. We are coining phrases based on Abba lyrics now. We have our very own in-house "Super Pooper".

We have our own lyrics as well. The most apt after a week of half term holidays might be:

> *"One of us is crying,*
> *cos one of us is lying*
> *and one of us is dying*
> *a slowww death stuck here in this fight that never never ends.*
> *One of us is lonely*
> *One of us is only*
> *Waiting for a time when she will be free to go out and have a break".*

So you have finished your psychology degree and now you are busily job hunting. Need any clients?

I am slowly building up the coaching – grown-ups and children. I am trying to bloom where I am planted, rather than look for a job in a coaching organisation or in HR. However, it all feels a bit Amway or Avon and I know I will not be convincing until I get over the fact that I am selling them something. Maybe ABBA will help – it brings back images of Mum buying Tupperware...

I think I texted you that Mum appears to have gone into remission but that they will do more chemo to consolidate that from the middle of November. I hope that it is the case that they did get it all. Apparently a biopsy is not a hundred percent accurate, but she is at home, resting and relaxing in between doctors' appointments, so for now we are all hopeful.

Hope Tim and the children are well – soon to be on summer

holidays – lucky things. We will be thinking of you as the nights draw in and the days grow colder and greyer here.

Much love and all our best wishes for your season – the exams, job hunting, hayfever, end of year break-up parties, Christmas and financial doom and gloom.

Tx

4 November, 2008

Dear Claire,

I hope you are well and enjoying having Mum at home with you. I sense she is very much living each day as it comes right now. How are you? Was the relief and the reprieve almost as exhausting as the worrying and waiting? I think I have been catching up on rest and finding a way to let out a lot of tension these past few days. I need only look in the mirror to find proof that all is not right with me.

I have a line of pimples across my brow running from left to right like little soldiers guarding my forehead. Maybe they are sentries, guarding the last frontier to my brain, or the border between the rational and the emotional. The usual legion on my chin has disappeared temporarily, also the company that took up a strategic position on my cheeks last month. But to be replaced by this new division? There must be a master plan somewhere in my endocrine system. A desire to ugly me into a change in diet or sleep patterns or brand of cleanser.

It's frightfully embarrassing at the tender age of 38 to have worse teenage acne than I had in adolescence. I am a like a poster girl for Clearasil – the "before" shots.

The children point the pimples out to me so diplomatically, saying: "What is that? Does it hurt?" They will have perfect skin like Andrew and his family, and one day my grandchildren will be asking me: "What is that pink sore on your chin Granny?".

Are you excited about the Melbourne Cup tomorrow? Taking the day off? I am waiting til it is time to call Dad and hear which horse to back. I know Mum was a punting up a storm from her hospital bed during the Caulfield Cup.

Apart from the skin problems we are all well. Andrew is back home tomorrow for a stretch of 5 days. We will cram in all the things normal people do over four months, like buy beds for the boys', clear up the autumn leaves in the garden, visit three sets of friends, have take away Indian food, maybe visit the accountant, go to china town and have a swim or two. It will be lovely for the boys to have him for a few days. I might go out one evening in tribute to the fact it is more than a 48 hour stop.

I have been writing a lot of letters to Mum, and am finding it very therapeutic to record my thoughts. I have an idea for a sitcom or a mini-series, themed around ordinary middle class people living their lives in the credit crunch era. If you would be my sounding board I would be so grateful.

Much love.

Tx

5 November, 2008

Dear Mum,

Sorry I have been out of touch for a few days. Not much news from us to report in any case. The boys are loving having their Daddy home – this time for 6 days. Tommy cried and whined the whole walk to school today – 20 minutes - that he wanted his Daddy – who sometimes walks with us when he is back. He was only consoled by the prospect of seeing Marta later in the day, for whom he then cried for the next 30 minutes. Sometimes I feel like an old dog, just some mangy old taken for granted pet that no one really misses or minds.

Between work, the children, setting up some coaching meetings and printing some advertising material, I have been pleasantly occupied. I have been reading some really good mystery novels by a Norwegian woman called Karen Fossum. She writes very evocatively, the characters are compelling, low key and really believable. Without any dramatic twists or turns, the plot plays out very tragically – yet realistically.

Had a lovely lunch today with a friend with whom I worked when I first came to London. Her husband is away half the time and we were sharing our experiences of being long distance spouses. We concurred that communication is the first thing to go, to be replaced by a sense of resentment and fatigue when they return, interloping in our space and separate life.

We then went to the gym together after lunch. I thought I had an arduous gym regime but lately it seems my body believes it is being starved and so it is laying down some hefty reserves for the winter. I am trying to spur it back to life with some interval training. I read somewhere that if you perspire a lot and easily it is an indication that you are really fit. I think this is bunkum, but if others have read it, it is doing my gym cred a world of good lately as I am sweating profusely in this bid to shift the autumn girth. While I could embrace the new me if it were just a kilo or two riding on the hips, the legion of pimples and the bad haircut and the Mumsy, transseasonal wardrobe worries, mean I am really starting to look like some credit crunch victim, a bag lady, or even a lonely washed up wife of an absent husband. It is a bit too much to embrace in one eight week period since returning from holiday in Australia.

I am trying to convince myself that my body is having a delayed reaction to the stress of worrying about you. Rather that, than having to accept that I have let myself go in this crazy time and my metabolism and fitness age has soared from a spry 33 to 53. I can't really talk about it to anyone else because that reveals a preoccupation with image that would invite confirmation that I do indeed look terrible. It would also reveal that I am not relaxed about everything after all, and I cannot afford for that image to fall away...

Last Sunday we were at our local café with another family who frequent it and the mother said to me how admiring she is of my calm state of mind with the boys and how great it is that I am so relaxed whenever she sees me out with them. I said that I am very used to them being out a lot and know their capacity to stay on the pavement and do as they're told, even when excited. I also explained that I am watchful and alert, despite my appearance. There are some things that always worry me and other things seem less important. I mean her kids probably love dogs and touch them whereas mine won't, through my training of them (the children, that is). That is not necessarily a sign of a relaxed person. Moreover, I am not so relaxed that I allow them to accept sweets from anyone, friend or stranger, without checking with me or a responsible person in loco parentis. Perhaps by having lots of ground rules that they follow, I have created a zone or sphere in which I do, as a result, feel quite calm.

Having said all of that, I won't be allowing sleep-overs til they are 20, apart from close family. To this a friend said that the statistics show that most molesters are uncles. What a chump. Not my children's uncles.

So on a happier note, Barack Obama is the new president of the USA. We are excited. It seems to herald a time of great possibilities and change for the better. While I know that you are very grateful not to be American, even though it is the best nation on earth, I hope that you also feel a sense of eager anticipation for the new era in store. We won't forget the date as it is the 5th of November which is imprinted in our brains due to the blasting and banging outside as neighbourhood pyromaniacs let off their firecrackers to celebrate Bonfire Night. The knowledge that a long grey winter lies ahead has the locals completely crazy around Halloween and Guy Fawkes. Once the last bonfire is doused but before the last jack-o-lantern is thrown in the compost pile, we start thinking about Christmas. I wonder if any recent thwarted act of terrorism or vigilantism will become the occasion for national partying 100 years from now. Maybe if it occurs in January or August? Nothing much happens then for the retail industry.

How are you feeling as you anticipate the next round of chemo? Is it all too horrid to even think about or is it in a perspective where you know you will endure it and be stronger afterwards?

I need to go now and watch some *NCIS*. It is so brilliant. I need a daily fix of it. I saw a website that said that while it is a well watched and well received series on the whole, the writer knew no one who watched it. I think that is due to the Friday and Saturday night scheduling. Only the oldies (not cyber aware so off the radar) and the losers are home to watch on those nights.

I will phone you tonight to hear your voice.

All our love.

Tx

PART THREE
The (beginning of the) End...

Email to Coaching Girls
6/11

Girls, I am thinking of organising a day conference for people who want to make a change of some sort but can't seem to take the first step. I sense that the first step is the blockage place. I know people who are interested in coaching and keen to have some, with time and money and inclination, but still keep making excuses that stop them from actually starting. It could be that the heart is not ready to embrace the changes that might become necessary. I think that there is some mileage to be made out of finding the way to unlock those issues.

Would you be interested in working with me to create this workshop which we could market in terms of confronting change in challenging times, with some sort of reference to the recession and transitions, say? We could get people brainstorming and interacting and making connections with a view to finding the keys to recession proofing your life; indeed, depression proofing your life.

If we create something savvy and cool and professional and get some corporate buy in – say retailers – maybe find a way to get some goody bags thrown in by someone holistic and environmentally responsible, we might get a really good attendance. We could each run a small subgroup where we group coach on a theme – e.g. happiness, sorting out values in difficult times, getting more out of yourself, finding the good intent in others, assertiveness and trusting one's voice.

I acknowledge that for some, the big issues might be handbags and haircuts, handsome men and botox. But that is the beauty of the happiness piece - the depression proofing agenda. We market it like some sort of recession busting tool kit, but in fact coach them all day on the things that matter to them. We throw in some champagne and good cheer at the end. I don't know about you but I would love that sort of workshop. What do you think?

As it's a one-off and involves some fun and treats – like a spa day with more - (I can see it becoming a bit girly as I write this), I think it might be attractive in the New Year anticlimax when no one has anything to look forward to. More compelling than the prospect of a series of financial hits over several weeks, that coaching might seem to involve.

I am really excited!

Let me know whether you are interested in helping take this forward.

T

7 November, 2008

Dear Bridget,

Great to hear that your trip to South America was so wonderful. Also that the return to work has been smooth and you are happy to be home.

I realise I have not been in touch for a while – not since my decedent trip to Paris to see Helen and family. Paris was lovely, as was my time with Helen. Thankfully, we all survived to tell the tale.

Thanks for checking out my websites. I now have the challenge of bringing in business. The recession doesn't help this at the moment, so I am conceiving new ways to get people to think about spending money on themselves. One idea is to run a workshop focussed on Happiness. I will naturally recommend *decedent* weekends away with friends as one means of enhancing pleasure...

A couple of weeks ago I was a little put out when, in relation to coaching children at school, my friend Lisa asked me: "What is your qualification to do this? What, you are a mum?" I nearly punched her, but stopped myself in time, as the boys were in the room. Instead I answered that as a trained coach, who debated for about a million years, and a lawyer, for whom making arguments and expressing them is second nature, I feel I have something to offer. Afterwards, I realised that I wanted to add that I have an imagination and enjoy children. Oh yes, and I actually think getting them to express themselves and think outside the box is important, and guess what, no-one else is clamouring to do this! The whole discussion actually triggered a bit of self doubt and questioning whether I really did have anything to offer.

Imagine! I did some self coaching and devised a little tool for reaffirming my self-belief.

It's really good to have the coaching vocabulary for what is essentially in such cases a really sophisticated form of denial and avoidance. Anyway, I am telling you this because you and I have often discussed the whole spectrum of denial and avoidance.

One of the knock-on effects of my fraudulent representation of myself as some sort of expert or guru, as Lisa would have one think, is that I have been asked to help with some children whose parents want to better manage sibling conflict and rivalry. Are we not all qualified on that front? I think the key is that no one needs to be the expert. If people "get" what coaching is about then they become very receptive to new ways of addressing challenges – i.e. they don't want to be fixed, but they want to grow and change things. It all comes down to mindset.

I hope your family is well and that you settle back in quickly. How is work? What does your role involve now? Any changes likely?

Tx

8 November, 2008

Dear Mum,

So grateful that you called with your news that you would not be going back to hospital for more chemo this week. I had a lot of time to think about you on Saturday night as I sat wretched and sweaty by the rubbish bin waiting to be ill. We went out to see some friends for the evening, dinner and company were both lovely, but I had a growing sense of doom as the minutes ticked by and the clock hands moved slowly past midnight. I was queasy and headachy and I knew the night would not end happily for me.

While it may have been a dodgy clam or some reaction to 2003 red wine (I am too ignorant to recall the name or the vineyard), or perhaps lobster for lunch (a rare day of extremely rich pickings), more likely it was Tommy's virus from last week. Anyway, I felt for you, as nausea and vomiting are just two of the side effects you have endured so uncomplainingly. I have to say the way I felt on Sunday, I would not wish chemo on anyone, let alone my dear Mummy. But I suppose we all have our preferred way of being ill. I don't want to tempt fate here, and of course some are worse than others, but as a rule I can live with a cold. And I do not seem to be prone to flu. But vomiting and hay fever are my sworn enemies.

Andrew, on the other hand, catches a sniffle every time he comes home and sneezes and coughs and hoiks the phlegm at such a rate and volume that you would honestly swear he was dying of emphysema, with hypertension and an imminent pulmonary embolism.

Enough of this though.

The great result was that I spent all of Sunday in bed resting and dozed for several hours, took a bath and read, while the boys were amused in the park, and going for a drive. I not only got rest and sympathy, I earnt lots of credit for my brave face on Monday morning when Andrew left for Lagos.

Meanwhile, I have been having lots of ideas about where to go with my coaching offering and initiatives. I am hosting the coffee morning next week to launch my workshops for women. I have had a reassuring rate of acceptances to the invitations that I printed and sent. I am now practicing what to say and how to say it to come over as both compelling and sincere, while also professional and expert. Should be a piece of cake.

On the whole, I have had both gratifying and disappointing receptions to my coaching business. Basically, the world can be divided into two camps – insofar as the world applies to me - of course.

In the first camp there are three sub-groups. First, there are the people who are close friends and revel and delight in the one's ideas and ventures and hope for the best in all things for one. The second category consists of good friends who are happy to hear about it and keen to be a part of something in some way. The third category are the well wishers and interested bystanders who feel no ownership or obligation to commit but whose response is warm and honest and interested.

The second camp consists of the close friends once removed. These are the women (unfortunately, it tends to be only women) who one thinks of fondly but whom one may not see as often, or who have drifted away due to circumstances or different interests. However, due to shared history or a former intimacy one tends to expect a level of warmth that equates with sub-group two of the first camp. And yet, one senses one cannot be truly open with them about certain things.

This category – while small – are powerful, because they have mastered the art of passive aggressive undermining. It is subtle, but very effective and powerful. There are members of this club who manage to pack so much meaning and tone into a single word or a look that one wishes one could bottle the emotion or spirit underpinning the remark or glance and sell it to the highest bidder as a secret weapon of mass destruction.

The well-timed quip and look of disbelief can set me right back. You may think I am hypersensitive and only want to hear positive reinforcing compliments. Perhaps. But it seems to me that when a person seems happy and engaged and full of energy it is rather churlish not to feel happy for them. It would certainly be good if I could hear unsupportive remarks and put them safely away in a place where they are benign and insignificant. To be mindful, I suppose; to just watch them pass me by.

In a self coaching moment of self challenge, I ask myself: what is the good intent behind feeling disappointed or let down by these friends? Can I look at the remark in another way and learn something from the degree to which it unsettles me?

Yes — as it happens. I find a table helps with this process...

Upsetting remark	Feeling	Good intent of the feeling?	Anything else?	Or...	How I now feel?
"Coaching? Really!? You go girl!"	Patronised.	I should not assume that what I do is of interest to everyone. Be more discerning when sharing my news.	Some people are not interested – accept it and move on.	Maybe it was not intended to be rude.	Better – it's only a remark.
No remark – complete denial that I have said or done anything - and a change of subject.	Small and irrelevant, disempowered and useless.	A reminder that I am, in fact, small and irrelevant.	Denial or refusal to engage may mean I am actually doing something right.	Perhaps the other person cannot engage at this time for their own reasons, but wishes they could.	A little indifferent, a little sympathetic.

"Physician – heal thyself."	Mixture of amused and deflated.	I should not get complacent or lose sight of my own learning needs.	Maybe it touches a nerve in the other person who, as yet, is not ready to change, or perhaps wishes they could.	It could be that I am a nutcase and no one else is honest or wise enough to see it and tell me.	Ah shit – who isn't a little loopy?
"What qualification do you have to run a club for kids – what - you are a mother?"	So annoyed.	It is useful for me to hear and reject self-limiting talk.	Lots of us feel we cannot do anything in case of failing.	By not seeing things in terms of qualification or success and failure one is free to try anything.	Look what one can do with a positive mindset.

Oh I forgot to tell you that I had a call from someone who saw my ad in the library. I now need to follow up with an email to her.

Now I am feeling much better.

Love you, speak soon.

Tx

14 November, 2008

Dear Mum,

I hope this letter reaches you in time for your birthday next week and before you return to hospital for the chemo. In any case I hope and pray that this round of treatment is not as severe in its side effects as the last one, and I hope you are home, well, and recovering by Christmas.

I have spent the week noticing the crumbs under the toaster and the water droplet marks all over the water filter jug, and the mildew on the skirting boards in the kitchen. As a rule these things don't really bother me – they are small irritations and can be addressed easily when one puts one's mind to it. However, with the imminent visit of 12 or more ladies on Tuesday, the state of my home is now a matter of urgent concern.

I have decided that I have some options as to how to play this. I can:

A) Mention in passing that I love the domestic chores and have no help because to get any would be a sacrifice. Consequently some things get missed.

B) Distract them from the greasy hand marks on the walls, and the bits falling off cupboards by a superb show of coaching and hospitality.

C) Quickly paint several canvasses in the next 72 hours and hang them in the messy kitchen so that they notice nothing else.

D) Try to relax. It might play to my advantage and make me appear more human and likeable as a coach, to have some rough edges in my domestic state.

I think I might apply a little of each of those options. I should also recognise that none of the people coming will be scrutinising my house for faults, or judging me if they do spot any.

Now all I need to do is to clean the rest of the flat and keep the boys from trashing it on the morning of the coffee session, prepare what I will say and hope that someone comes prepared to be coached in front of 11 other women.

I am also tempted to gauge their interest for a full day seminar. I am tossing up between an elegant and spoiling "spa day for the mind and soul" or a very pragmatic, down to earth, "back to basics" workshop.

I have been perusing the corporate messages surrounding our departmental "vision" and "way" and "purpose" that have been published at work this past week. The predecessor of the "vision" was the "ambition" but I gather it was not very stretching and a staff survey revealed that everyone was so in touch with, and actually living, the "ambition" that it had to be abandoned. It can't be an ambition if it is a reality, you see. So now we have a vision which is a far more uplifting and reach for the stars aspiration. And yet day to day life seems more or less unchanged.

This is its purpose:

"Whatever role you're in, you make judgements on how to behave and how to make decisions. If you know the Vision, you'll know how to act. If everyone understands the Vision and lives it then we'll make better judgements and better decisions."

This makes good sense – having a vision does tend to help one to think clearly.

It makes me feel very much part of something great though. I want to incorporate or adapt the "vision" to my business and home life. I wonder if the boys would be happy to be part of it. Maybe we can fashion our own little message and decorate it and have it at the front door like we do at work.

We can choose colours and fonts and illustrate it really nicely.

I think something along the lines of "Stickers are the best reward around" might go down well. Or "chips, doughnuts and sweets rule". So our purpose becomes "to act in ways that get us more of these good things, while "having fun" (Jack's mantra) and "doing your best" (mine), and with well brushed teeth (Daddy). This is something quite compelling. But we also need a "way" - "to spoil another's fun while evading capture and scolding, but wherever possible, spilling glitter and small cars everywhere one goes".

The "way" is actually very hard to pin down. I think this is a misnomer – actually haven't read the office "way" yet - and can't really determine what the idea of a corporate "way" is really getting at – unless it is a typo and should read the weigh, or the wane... or maybe it's the wine, or the whine.

Loads of love and happy birthday, dear Mummy.

Tx

17 November, 2008

Dear Mum,

Glad you received the flowers in time for your birthday and so that you have a couple of days enjoyment of them before they become contraband and forbidden due to the infection risk in the cancer ward.

I was cleaning the kitchen cupboard and sorting out mugs for the coffee morning and found that I could not remove two mugs – they seemed to be stuck to the shelf. I got up on a chair to take a closer look, thinking maybe they were put away unclean and a sticky rim was to blame. Nothing so innocent, it seems. Rather, someone – clearly with access to my home and my shelves and time alone in the flat – has superglued the cups to the shelf.

Who would do such a thing?

Motive, opportunity?

Opportunity excludes everyone except nannies. We have no other people in the property without us. Motive? Have I really pissed one off that much? We have only had four in 7 years so – which one?

I should be glad that no harm befell my children given someone felt malicious enough to glue two mugs down. So passive aggressive! I completely understand, and embrace, passive aggressive behaviour! Who hasn't had a row with the spouse and wanted to destroy his favourite tie or CD? I remember the time I threw Andrew's ridiculous talcum powder out of a window into a light well in a fit of pique – knowing he would eventually see it and think he had done it himself or it had fallen by accident. He did neither actually.

He asked me outright whether I had knocked it out the window on purpose. You see what I have to put up with? As I could not feign ignorance I had to admit to accidentally knocking it out the window while cleaning.

But to secretively and with malice aforethought, stand on a chair and take out enough cups from the front of the shelf to make a space for the victim cups, and then carefully stick them down, replace the front cups and wait for the day when I notice? What a gamble this child care game can be, eh? Some borderline personality has been wilfully damaging my home to make, or not make, a point.

Of the two possible culprits, one seemed happy to the end when she left to care for her sick mother (that old chestnut), the other was seldom alone in the house as she lasted but a month. She secretly took my boys to Ikea so that she could buy a new shower head – a 60 minutes journey on three types of public transport - brought her own son over more days than not, and finally resigned by text in a fury when I asked her to give me more notice if she knew she could not come to work.

I tell you this Mum – it will teach me to spring clean! Goodness knows what other little surprises may be lurking at the bottom of a pile of papers or at the back of a cupboard.

Just because I am paranoid doesn't mean the nannies aren't out to get me. I hope I am not laying blame in the wrong place, though. Perhaps Andrew secretly harbours some resentments...

We attended a kiddies' birthday party yesterday. The host was saying that the entertainer charged £300 for two hours of his games and music. I was amazed. I could do that with both hands tied behind my back. I cannot charge that much for coaching and would hate to charge that for legal advice, and here is some guy in a Superman costume – not that super, I hasten to add – milking it for all it's worth.

What a great way to make a living. The only downside is time away from the family on weekends. And then again – maybe that's not so bad. The kids at these parties are always captivated, no one ever says – "gee, crap entertainer this time", the parents aren't exactly fussed as long as the little tykes are occupied and not running around crazy, damaging the venue, and if they are any good, the entertainer is basically being paid to advertise his or her services to a captive audience of future and potential clients.

This is the fundamental underpinning ethos of my coaching coffee morning – show them what you can do – they will buy it. Tell them and they will walk away unconvinced. I need to somehow repackage my children's coaching idea into a party entertainment offering. Maybe a debate party? Would that be too nerdy? Would people just laugh? Why not? It's not like it would not be fun! I would have gone to that sort of party – willingly. I know I was a swot and loved to be in the limelight – but there must be children or parents, like that out there for whom this sort of entertainment would be compelling. Also, from my point of view as the "talent", a debate party would be a great deal less labour and prop intensive than say, a dance or theatre party. I know I could not deal with all those girls wanting to be the princess; all the boys who want to do a sword fight.

But a debate party or an argument party would be fantastic. I know you are thinking – who needs a theme party anyway? Can't the parents just let them play or organise a few games for them? No Mum. Times have changed. I might put it out there in the teeny-bopper marketplace and see what happens. I need to find a wealthy American family of lawyers, nostalgic about their high school debate days, who are really keen to push their kids and differentiate themselves...

Love

Tx

19 November, 2008

Dear Mum,

The coffee and coaching morning was a success. I enjoyed it immensely and learnt a lot about group dynamics and how to go about structuring my group workshops to maximise the coaching benefits. There was a lot of interaction and some really good questions about how coaching differs from counselling, and what sort of topics it could focus on. I did a coaching session that demonstrated the process at play and I think everyone got something out of it. We shall see whether anyone books to attend the workshops. I suspect, like everything in the business process so far, it will start slow and snowball into something reasonable as time goes by.

One of the guests made some remarks about clinical psychology. It was quite thought provoking – namely the way in which coaching can and does trespass in areas that may once have been the exclusive domain of counselling or other therapies. We were able to draw out some distinctions, of course. Clearly the man in the street does not need or turn to counselling for career transition advice, nor does one usually think of seeking counselling in managing matters before they reach a crisis or crunch time. I am not undermining the work of psychologists at all and I really appreciate and value the enormous assistance psychology brings to coaching in understanding why and how people are as they are. However, people who are looking to change something or breakthrough a behaviour or mindset that gets in their way, do not tend to think about seeing a counsellor or therapist.

I have now learnt a little more about the business of coaching within organisations as well. I received a call from a coaching company who asked me to send them my bio – biographic details – for them to refer to a client (a law firm) that is looking for a third party coach. I was excited at the prospect! I was a little thrown by the idea of a bio. It seems this is a couple of paragraphs about one's background. I sent them something that described who I am as a coach – a sort of pitch or ethos document. I was told this was not suitable and they wanted a *biography* of me as a coach. Apparently, this is a term of art and devising one is quite a feat.

The upshot is that in a biography one makes really wide sweeping statements as to the extent and depth of one's expertise in very broadly defined categories – communication and management and interacting with counterparties – and then one drops the names of all the clients and targets one has worked with. One then refers to one's former identify before one took the life changing steps of becoming a coach. One can see why psychologists might have an issue with coaches.

A bio is essentially a form of self promoting advertising. Who will check the claims made? After I modified my bio to be fit for purpose, it seemed very bland indeed and I did not really recognise myself. Of course, coaches with expertise in certain sectors have a great brand and lots of experience – by definition. And of course one needs to sell that to potential clients. But what is not communicated with a bio is who you are and what differentiates you from the hundreds of other self promoting experts in that same field. After all, if organisations are looking for coaches there is a good chance their motivation is to improve management of staff or communication with customers or clients. By definition then, the coach is coming to deal with *communication* and *management* issues. That's pretty much the spectrum. So if all corporate coaches can help with these issues – and of course they can – it's their bread and butter, how does a potential client choose based on these anodyne bios that all proclaim expertise in communication and management?

Is it by having a whizzy website? Or having really top drawer clients? Is it the academic pedigree of its coaches? Every one of those can be seen as both a plus and a minus. An experienced coach observer and mentor on my course commented that organisations are looking for great coaches, not failed lawyers and ex-bankers. How do they know who is a great coach then? Word of mouth, referrals, price and number or "quality" of other clients? But the corporate client must not be told anything personal or meaningful. There must be no shared or common philosophy or sense of values or humour, at least not in the bio or pitch. It seems that one can find out more about one's hairdresser or handy man than one's coach.

Anyway I did what was asked. What do I know about getting clients?

I hope the return to hospital is not too miserable and that the chemo all starts and progresses without event.

Missing you all.

Love

Tx

22 November, 2008

Dear Claire,

How is Mum? Let me know if things get rough. How is work? All is well here. Given our recent chats about psychology and your perspectives on therapy given your experiences with schizophrenia among homeless people, I wanted to tell you I am keen to run a Happiness Workshop next year. The idea behind it is to help people to focus on and be grateful for the good things in their lives, and to gain clarity and perspective on the less positive areas or the aspects they would like to change. While it comes on the back of the women's workshops that I was telling you about on the phone last week, I would like it to be pretty broad sweeping in its appeal and effect. Not a gimmicky miracle workshop that will solve all your problems, but a safe place to share ideas and get back to basics. The current mood in the market place is very much oriented to cutting out the excess and trimming the fat from one's life. A seminar that ties into that agenda and helps people to clarify their priorities and identify ways of achieving realistic goals that actually further their long term happiness would be quite appealing. We all know what makes us happy: the right mix of good and nurturing relationships, fun and pleasant pursuits, being loved and cared for, a fulfilling job or project. I want to get the attendees to refocus on these sources of joy and fulfilment, while giving them the option to also develop new ways of seeing their lives. I personally ascribe many forms of unhappiness or malaise to misplaced or disappointed expectations. If we could get *real* about what we want we would be some way towards a happier state of mind.

It seems very simple and obvious, but even a few conversations with friends and colleagues suggests that there is a huge demand for literature or training that assists people in search of greater happiness, more fulfilment. I think in these times where we are all tightening our belts and wondering about jobs and the housing market and the value of investments, working out what makes us really happy is fundamentally important. This is a basic and obvious and universal quest but it tends to be distorted and clouded and morphed out of all recognition by advertising and media hype, tabloid sensationalism, consumerism and commercialism and obsessions with brand names and status. People seem not to know what they really need in order to feel good every day. They wonder why the thrill of a new handbag wears off, why the benefits of a luxury holiday are not longer lasting.

The newspapers publish Rich Lists and Power Lists. The magazines print Style guides and rankings of the most glamorous, sexy and influential. Yet, for real people, such is entirely irrelevant. Sure, it can be interesting, diverting and entertaining to know who controls Hollywood or the runways of Milan. And of course, it is big business. But neither that knowledge nor the insidious repercussions of it, in terms of what is stocked in the high street stores, or who is representing which perfume brand, matter in the pursuit of happiness by ordinary people.

It is time the media jumped on a new bandwagon and published the Happy List and the Sensible List and the Most Sorted and Generous lists. If you have any idea for workshop topics let me know.

Speak soon.

Tx

23 November, 2008

Dear Mum,

I wanted to write and tell you about my lovely week. I have been so inundated with positive ideas and support from all quarters. It has been very enriching and rewarding; from the coffee morning which has yielded two clients and a coaching assignment to work with some children, as well as positive feedback, to the ideas I put to the school for more play based coaching for children. I have also caught up with friends who I have not seen for some months.

My reading has broadened my perspective on communicating with my own children and dealing with the bickering and meltdowns. I was called into the fray this evening and I suggested the boys reach their own resolution as I felt confident they could and wanted to. And they did.

Bring on the next problem guys!

So what about you? I almost don't want to call in case you are having an awful time already and feeling nauseous and woozy – as you were around this time last treatment.

How is my Dad? Give him our love.

I had a moment of serendipity yesterday. During my afterschool communication club with the 10 year olds I was focussing on the use of humour to convey messages. I contextualised this by referring to advertising so as to illustrate how humour helps to bond us and break down barriers, and can make a message more memorable. I asked the children to make up some little ads for products of their choosing; the key task was to use humour to persuade us of the merits of their product. I suggested that in doing so, a link between unrelated things can give a product an appeal or identity that grabs our attention.

After the class Jack and I went home via the supermarket for milk and honey and the Thursday evening treat of crisps. He chose a brand that had a picture of a cannon on the packet. Jack said: "What has a cannon got to do with salt and vinegar crisps?" Admittedly, Jack is the last person advertisers and brand managers need to target in their quest to sell these tasty, salty delights. But clearly even a six year old is not duped by pointless packaging. Moreover, the key factor in determining a good packet of crisps was not satisfied with the cannon ones – the pack was small and half empty.

Jack is pretty astute, but not more so than many children, I suspect. So what happens to people as they age? Is the assault of advertising and product placement so vicious that this discernment is beaten out of us after years and years of exposure?

Many of the products we buy are never advertised. The best tasting grocery items and the most effective household products are not widely marketed. Definitely a nice looking package helps with shelf appeal, just like a good cover on a book raises our interest. But actual advertisements often miss the mark. Maybe I am anomalous in my purchasing habits, because I am struggling to think of a single ad that has influenced me to buy a product. Oh – I just thought of one – Floor Wipes.

I freely admit that research or press commentary can impact my purchasing decisions. Only yesterday I ordered six books due to the press surrounding the Roald Dahl Funny Book prize. Also, word of mouth can work wonders. I had never heard of Primark (a very inexpensive "fashion" store) until I started going to playgroup. The mothers rave about it. Similarly when one told me about a store that sells reduced price brands I made a special trip to buy a large coffee percolator. No ad could compel a similar effort.

I found some research on the web about the psychology of advertising and its impact.

"We have reason to assume that the best, most effective advertising for a product is not found in the official advertising reserves, but in everyday life.

The best advertising for a cigarette is when a work colleague lights one up in a stress situation and subsequently finds a more relaxed work rhythm. The best advertising for a beer is the facial expression of the person next to the drinker after he takes a sip. And the best advertising for a car make is the new car of a friend.

It is regrettable that researchers and creative people pay so little attention to this everyday advertising. For every individual has developed great artistry in day-to-day advertising, and this has been exploited much too little."[6]

In fact, for me, the more airplay a product gets, the more common and unspecial it feels. The idea that high prices reflect quality is questionable. One is buying an idea, an image or an emblem, not a product. Even if it costs a small fortune – how special can it be if everyone has one? Why am I wasting your time with this? Because this pressure to acquire more stuff on the promise that it will make us happy, or more desirable – and thus happy - is the source of all this wanton consumption and so much unhappiness. I am tossing it around as it seems that it would be a good topic for my happiness seminar. We need to acknowledge that the pressure to conform to external images of success, stylishness or accomplishment is making life harder not better.

I have finally completed my course work for the coaching programme and am ready to submit it. Oh I chuckled knowingly when the course director remarked that some people never bother to submit their work and thus never receive their certificates. And here I am, five months later finally sending away my portfolio.

---

6 Rheingold Institute for Qualitative Market and Media Research, Article " The Psychology of Advertising Impact", 2008.

This is what I wrote. You will think I have joined a cult:

Assessment of my learning as a coach

Looking back over the learning journey which I anticipated at the outset, and as documented in my journal, I am amazed at how smooth and sure the road has been. The learning has been immense and the journey very exciting and stimulating. I was not expecting rough territory or insurmountable challenges, but the odd upset or set back seemed to be a reasonable expectation.

In fact I am not sure that there have been any real set-backs at all. I felt throughout the course a profound "rightness" that what I was learning made sense and helped me as a coach. I felt that I was enlightened with so much information that enabled me to develop and to learn, while at the same time, now at the end, it seems as if I always knew it. The content of the programme was so sensibly and artfully structured and layered as to make the journey very intuitive and natural.

So while I learnt a great deal and now have a huge resource in terms of theory and analytical background and research to draw upon, it all makes very good sense. One could almost risk diminishing the learning that has gone on.

I recall several key themes along the way – after the first module I felt confident and buoyant, freed and inspired. It seemed that I could listen and build rapport. After the second module I felt connected with my peers and appreciated for who I am as a person. This was enabling and empowering. After the third module, I was aware of a desire to be more present and to achieve a "dance in the moment" with a client. I was struck by the impact that receiving feedback had on some people. This inspired me to try to better understand the processes different people have when receiving feedback or criticism. By June I was crying out for more rigour and intensity. I was role playing and daring to dream, using a voice I had

ZOË COPLEY

quieted some time ago. I was finding that as my non-coaching persona was able to express new things in new ways, my coaching persona was able to be still and present more and more. Finally, during the fifth module, the whole thing seemed to coalesce. When one of the participants was coaching me and asked me whether she, as a client, would know she had "been Tess'ed" I recognised what I had previously only hoped for - that the personal journey and the coaching journey were inextricably linked in a very positive way.

By being coached, the learning journey to become a coach is made so much richer and multifaceted. I have discovered new resources and talents within myself, some of which I had previously diminished or failed to appreciate. I have galvanised an energy that I used to envy in peers and colleagues. I have connected with the unspoken wish in people in a new way. I feel privileged to be able to share in their journeys, albeit only for an instant. It follows that I truly know that coaching can liberate and inspire, engage and transform in both a meaningful and immediate way.

Coaching is indeed a means for us to become our best selves. My journey has been both a grounding, and at the same time, uplifting experience. It has been thoroughly rewarding and I am delighted that this journey has begun. I know I have barely scratched the surface of the learning that lies in store for me.

I can hear you thinking – "oh God. That's great, love".

I hope the side effects have not started to present – though I expect some will have by the time this reaches you. I hope in any case that you will be over it very quickly and that your white cells and neutrophils recover as well as they did last time. Hopefully you will be home for Christmas.

Much love to you and all the family.

Tx

26 November, 2008

Dear Mum,

I hope you are continuing to feel well with so few side effects and no infections. I will speak with you or Dad later tonight and hear how things are progressing.

I have been considering running a seminar about happiness and have been looking into what this might involve. I have to preface this with the comment that I am doing this based on a belief that people want to be happy. I do not say this is all they want or that they want it all the time. I do think, though, that fundamentally we have come to expect or desire that we achieve happiness at least part of the time. Naturally there are other wants and desires as well – power, fame, money, popularity, to leave a mark. But to some extend the desire for happiness underpins these. People think the power, or fame or notoriety will make them happy. I don't think I can run a seminar on how to get powerful or notorious, in any event. What I do think though is that people are interested in feeling good about themselves and their choices. They may not know exactly what they want or how to get it. They may think they want something only to achieve that and feel no better, no happier. They may think they know exactly what they want but feel they cannot get it. They may lack know-how or energy or motivation or willpower. Whatever the case, they have a pretty good idea that they liked it the time or times that they felt good, happy and relaxed.

Assuming then that people are interested in happiness per se, I am grappling with how to approach such a huge concept. I am conscious that the very question begs so many more. Questions like

– can it be defined, or quantified? How do we know it when we feel it? Is it realistic to expect to be happy? Do high expectations jeopardise happiness or inspire harder work towards securing it? Can we control whether we are happy? Is it a question of faith? Does it all come down to genes and personality? Should we even ask these questions while there are millions for whom basic human needs are not met – food, water, sanitation? If we can be happy in isolation from others, irrespective of others, then what does it say about happiness as a virtue? Is happiness moral?

It is clear that I will have to focus on one or two angles in order to create a useful workshop.

I want to share with you some data I have been reading in what is called the "science of happiness" – the realm of positive psychology. The essence can be captured in the following quote from an article by Claudia Wallis in *Time Magazine* on January 17, 2005.

(University of Pennsylvania psychologist Martin Seligman in his 2002 book Authentic Happiness) "finds three components of happiness: pleasure ("the smiley-face piece"), engagement (the depth of involvement with one's family, work, romance and hobbies) and meaning (using personal strengths to serve some larger end). Of those three roads to a happy, satisfied life, pleasure is the least consequential, he insists: "This is newsworthy because so many Americans build their lives around pursuing pleasure. It turns out that engagement and meaning are much more important."

It was Seligman who had summoned the others to Akumal that New Year's Day in 1998, his first day as president of the American Psychological Association (A.P.A.) to share a vision of a new goal for psychology."I realized that my profession was half-baked. It wasn't enough for us to nullify disabling conditions and get to zero. We needed to ask, what are the enabling conditions that make human beings flourish? How do we get from zero to plus five?"

What a lovely lot of common sense. It seems that in 10 short years an entire new body of psychology has emerged. As a result, many have jumped on the bandwagon and there are in fact dozens of courses, books and downloadable resources all telling us "how to be happy". One theory is that happiness is 50% attributable to genes, 8% attributable to circumstances (home, marriage, wealth) while the rest is down to the "slings and arrows" of life[7]. There is a conflict between some researchers who claim that the end point of an experience determines how much pleasure we derive from it and another school of thought that says that the experience itself is less meaningful than the memory of it. By the latter, I expect they mean that how we choose to store and draw on the memory is the key, and that is not so much the driver of our happiness as a symptom of our personality and genes and approach to life. I tested this out among my afterschool communication club today – to a child they all agreed that given a choice they would prefer normal life with their memory intact over a year of perfect happiness that they would not be able to remember.

I even found scientific research to support my ranting about advertising. According to Mark Easton, BBC reporter- "The science of happiness suggests advertising is a major cause of unhappiness because it makes people feel less well-off.[8]"

It's fascinating reading. The best part is just how happy all of the world experts in positive psychology appear in their photos on their websites. They have *me* convinced. Not only because what they say is eminently sensible, but because they are also making a difference, bridging the gap between theory and practice, science and day-to-day life for real people.

I too feel that I am a walking, talking example of what Seligman says. I have felt over the past few months very happy and very

7 David Lykken University of Minnesota,1996, quoted by Claudia Wallis in Time Magazine," The New Science of Happiness", 17 January 2005. Lykken has since revised his views, according to Wallis who quotes him as saying to Time: "It's clear that we can change our happiness levels widely—up or down."
8 News.bbc.co.uk. The science of Happiness, 30 April 2006, Mike Rudin.

engaged. Great friendships and family got me part of the way but the pursuit of hobbies like the gym and cinema did not ensure that sense of rightness and contentment. Now, with a sense of purpose and some engagement of the mind and spirit and the will, comes a far more lasting and permanent sense of joy. So while spending time with friends, sipping cappuccinos and watching the world go by from an Italian café or jogging on the beach at Tugun are all sources of pleasure, longer lasting happiness requires meaningful and engaging activity. It is arguable that all of those things are in fact pleasant as well as meaningful and engaging.

It tallies with your view that you get out of life what you put into it. I should acknowledge Andrew's views too, as ever since I first met him, he has insisted that productivity and meaningful and engaging work is the key to happiness. Work, per se, may be limiting or too narrow. The analysis would seem to permit a fairly subjective view of what is engaging and pleasant.

All of this is quite timely, as I have had a number of interesting conversations over the past few days with people feeling anything but happy. The source of their discontent is fairly specific – the men in their lives.

In one case the issue comes down to being lied to, taken for granted and generally messed around. In the other case the issue pertains to a mismatch in expectations of what life should be at this time and a sense that life is passing her by.

However, the theme that permeated both situations was a sense that the woman was totally without control or power over her own destiny. I was struck by a feeling that both of them were deeply isolated and lonely. Their respective confusion and frustration was starker because what seemed to be obvious solutions, were to them, unworkable. What was also stark was their belief that they could not, or would not, say certain things to the relevant man, for fear of the ramifications for them if they did.

Well, we have all been there. Many times have I felt that sense of pointlessness when contemplating broaching topics with Andrew. And yet without the communication taking place, the feelings of desperate isolation and uncertainty can often increase. I must say that absence is a wonderful tool to assist in the mending and binding of one to one's partner in certain key ways. I find I am grateful Andrew comes home at all, grateful he doesn't sleep the entire time he is home and delighted to be hearing about another place and another world removed from that which I inhabit.

After seeing both of these friends, I was reading the press coverage of some celebrity divorces. It can take mere seconds to be granted a decree nisi and be free and clear.

As I have never really looked into the ins and outs of getting a divorce I was not aware that one gave grounds for the split, when petitioning for divorce. I know that no fault divorce is available, though if I were to explore the divorce options down the track, I would expect that a no fault situation would not be pertinent. Nevertheless, it was both reassuring and disconcerting to read that one basis is "unreasonable behaviour". This is a lovely catch-all euphemism. No dirty laundry need be aired. So British.

One of the UK's greatest exports; an entrepreneur/ restaurateur/celebrity chef, has been exposed as a long term philanderer. The mothers at playgroup were shocked and amazed to read this. I truly fear that I am incapable of being shocked by some things. Sure, the remarkable interest Andrew can show in the new Mercedes G Wagon is a little shocking. But when it comes to reports in the paper I seem to have lost all sense of decorum. Only the most horrific stories of abuse and torture, mayhem, poverty and destruction seem to affect me. Oh, and there is something poignant and emotive about the Barack Obama factor, but these sordid tales of marital disharmony and infidelity barely dent my consciousness. It is as if I always knew he was having an affair. Perhaps I need to look more closely at myself and the underlying assumptions I am making about celebrity, public personalities and indeed, certain types of men.

I do not suggest that everyone is out there searching for an illicit romp, but we are so often exposed to the idea – press, TV, movies, royal family, celebrities, politicians - that the impact of such news is not immense. I know it sounds cynical and perhaps smug to say: I am not that surprised. But seriously, a restaurant brand and fortune in excess of £65 million? Would he really not be in the way of a lot of stress, temptation and opportunity? Statistically it is quite likely that a person in his position will stray from his marriage. Given circumstances, pressures we know nothing of within and without the marriage, as well as huge media attention, a gruelling schedule and plenty of eager women in his way, at the best of times, is it any wonder?

I am not excusing the behaviour. But it is not for the public and the media to come over all high and mighty. We run the risk of being sanctimonious hypocrites. It is not a happy tale. It is easy to spin it to make good copy and to editorialise on it, but is it really necessary? So he misled his public. Well would he really announce that he was having an affair? So he is not squeaky clean. Who is? So he is not the great family man he has conned us into thinking he was? Did he con us, or did we let ourselves believe whatever we wanted to believe? Why do we put so much stock in his marriage and the age and names of his kids, in the first place? It may be a big con, but not of his making. The whole thing: the media beat up, the branding and merchandising of talent, the caché that aspirational Londoners attach to dining in one of the myriad starred eateries, and now the fall from grace. I feel sorry for them.

There but for the Grace of God...

Back to the wider issue of unhappiness. So is there a solution to relationship stress and misery? A salve for the disappointment? Given that prevention is better than cure, I have been trying to come up with more useful ways of testing compatibility with a potential spouse than the ones relied on heretofore. I mean, couples live together, play together, work together and generally know each other quite well before they tie the knot. And yet still relationships fail. We expect that they will be tested, given the vicissitudes of life, after all. But they still fracture. Is one cause the expectations with which we embark on partnership? Another, our expectation that we *must* be happy. Fundamentally, there is a lot that people do not know at the time they make the commitment. Hence the lamentations of "He is not the man I married"; "If I had known he was such a chauvinist/womaniser/workaholic/alcoholic/bore/golf-crazed lunatic/mummy's boy/couch potato – I would never have married him".

Women seem stumped when they find the partner does not step up or deliver in certain key ways. Often the evidence was there all along, but they could not see it or have it pointed out to them, or they believed that time and their influence might change him.

So, what if more of those challenging situations and scenarios that expose the dud qualities that so disappoint and enrage later on, could be explicitly brought to light in the early period? So much heartache and heartbreak might be avoided. The punters could assess more critically and with better information whether to bail at the early stage. On the other hand, the eyes would be open sooner to the risk areas and steps could be taken to mitigate or manage them, or even to foster communication, change or counselling. But even more usefully perhaps, the boring guys would come into their own. Those blokes that seem so dull and ordinary, would be afforded a chance to shine and to impress, as their less obvious but enduring qualities might triumph, given the right sort of challenge.

What I envisage is a couples testing ground. A series of challenges or questions that help unearth the real person who in later life or crisis situations, will prove reliable and solid or unsuitable.

It would be the antithesis of speed dating: rather, slow dating. People would take their time and do proper old fashioned due diligence, using a really testing questionnaire to discern whether their partner has what they are looking for, followed by a gruelling series of tasks. It could even become a method of finding a partner. At one end of the spectrum I could conceive of an "Apprentice" for Loved Ones, say. How would it work? I create a series of tasks that allow the client to observe their partner in their natural, competitive, uncontrived and purest forms. Fighting for survival (due to cash prizes), we could assess their potential in areas that come to matter most. I am not sure yet whether it would work, commercially, or on a large scale. However, in a smaller workshop style environment where competition might be kept at bay, the clients could better assess the real potential of their relationship.

It occurs to me that it would work better as a means of assessment of risk areas and stress areas that lie dormant, awaiting the trigger event to awake and drive couples asunder. Maybe all I am really designing is a couples coaching service – a pre-emptive means of addressing these issues before they drive a wedge between them. It is not far from what the Catholic Church tries to do with its pre-marriage classes for engaged couples. There's a thought! I could develop a questionnaire, frame it in terms of marriage preparation and offer it to the Church.

A questionnaire would start the ball rolling and provide a point of reference for coaching. Having said that, I can't imagine too many engaged blokes rushing off to the EC (engaged couples) coach on Friday night. Suffice to say, if my fiancé were really into it, I would start having doubts.

So a questionnaire or assessment process to counterbalance the combined impact of having an abundance of the natural human tendency to hope for the best, to be incapable of taking constructive criticism and to be deliriously in love (if not a little desperate to be married).

The "Love-is-not-Blind" Questionnaire – helping the intelligent person to see dispassionately and objectively just what they are getting into.

On that cheery note I will wish you a speedy return home – though not too speedy – better to be handy to the antibiotics and infection free wards than exposed to the humid and germ filled air of the suburbs...

Much love.

Tx

27ᵗʰ November, 2008

Dear Mum,

Dad told me you were going along very well so far and no side effects to speak of. I am sorry I have not called for 4 days. The time has slipped by very fast.

Not much to report from here. The weather is very cold, though a little more temperate today than the past few days. The children are schizophrenic in their behaviour; bickering and squabbling one minute, loved up with a new imagination game the next. The magic combination of missing Daddy, tiredness, dark winter days, long anticipation of Christmas, each of them coming to a peculiarly strong willed stage in their own development and a bizarre desire to look for attention in any way or form had me ragged by this morning. So after dinner I convened a meeting to establish what exactly the problems were. It seemed to alleviate the tension and take the wind out of their sails. I wrote down the grievances without comment, then summarised our desired outcome and actions. We now have a list of good behaviours that we need to work towards. For example: no more hitting or name calling; use words not screams. Jack then told me to add: Do as Mummy says the first time.

I have brain washed them completely now...

Some of the happiness research I mentioned[9] referred to data drawn from a survey of 700 Texan women asked to rank the things that gave them happiness. Taking care of children was way down on the list – just above housework. I was surprised by that – vacuuming is one of my

---

9 www.authentichappiness.sas.upenn.edu

greatest sources of pleasure. Nothing beats getting those curly grey dust bunnies out of the corners of the stairs or the satisfying chink, clink, tttt sound as the toast crumbs are sucked up the wand. If one is savvy the children are enlisted to help, as their eager little hands love nothing more than wiping off layers of dust on dark surfaces. Also, I find that if I act really reluctant to let them help then they want to even more.

I want to do some of the many happiness focussed questionnaires on the Authentic Happiness website but now I fear that if I do participate in the surveys I may skew the results, as I derive a lot of pleasure from unconventional things. Shopping is very low on my list of happy pursuits; as is eating out. Reading probably outranks everything, closely followed by time with friends; though time with friends and family – including children - is higher than everything else. One constantly hears people say that if they had to spend more time with their children they would go mad. Or they only enjoy their children in small doses, or school holidays are too long. What would they rather do? Work?

There is a way out if you need it though. Tommy is currently running around the house calling out –"you are my enemy Mummy". It is entirely plausible that our aggrieved upstairs neighbour who already thinks I am a crazy fishwife, will tip-off child services. We will face an investigation into why my sons speak as they do to me. Between Felix calling me a pig (I agreed Tommy could have his toy dog back), Tommy yelling – "all of us are cryin'" and Jack's amateur theatrics in Sainsbury's with "I'm baking you (begging) pleeeeeesssse can I have some crisps!" I risk them being shipped off into care.

Be nice to have the place to myself for a while though...

Speaking of which, I have finalised the "Love-Is-Not-Blind" questionnaire. I will attach it with my next letter for your perusal.

Much love

Tx

29 November, 2008

Dear Mum

It was good to hear your voice this morning. You sounded very well and strong. If they have put chemo drugs in you then it appears your system is not yet feeling it. I hope it continues in this vein (pardon the pun).

I have had a fun day. Had my afterschool club today and team meeting at work, a lovely walk home from school with Jack and a crazy evening. Sadly the OMG (old married guy) at the gym has been sidelined out of a job as the new department head in his government organisation has advertised and filled the role OMG was acting in for the past year with someone from outside the wider department. It is a huge shame as he – OMG - was doing a great job, was very well qualified for the role and as the incumbent, would normally be pretty much assured of getting the permanent role.

You may remember I met OMG when I first came to the UK to work and he was a source of great wisdom and friendship during those weird times when I was adjusting to living in London and I had all those ideas about making the law better and clearer and easier to use. We had many philosophical discussions and debates about the law, the courts and our responsibilities as lawyers. I was young and idealistic and full of ideas and a longing for reform. OMG was jaded-realistic. It was my then flat mate, Pat, who had given him the pseudonym "OMG" and it has stuck since, even now, all these years later. Anyway he is now out of a job because of the jobs for the other boys situation that has played out against him. You know how I hate favouritism and nepotism. It is the way of the world, but for all the good it may do one or two people it does an awful lot of harm to others and to the minions that see it playing out before them. Meritocracy. Mmm. I am no further along now than when I began writing these letters to you. A little more phlegmatic, but still perturbed to some extent, by the fact that politics and power plays and who one knows, counts for more than what one knows or who one is.

I know that it is "life". At every level in every corridor; Whitehall, Threadneedle St, the schoolyard, the buses. The totalitarian regime that exists on some bus routes is tantamount to life in Mussolini's Italy. Even the distribution of roles for the school Christmas play can be a jackpot based not on ability, poise, confidence or motivation, but some secret arbitrary matrix of favour, mother's influence, gender, personality and classroom behaviour, hair colour and cuteness. I won't open up that can of worms though. I overheard it being done to death in the ladies change room at the gym the other day. It seems insignificant but is in fact vitally important as the play can produce some of our proudest moments, eh? Remember when Daniel was the narrator in his year 7 speech night production of "Joseph"?

On a happier note, I have set out my "Love-is-not-Blind" Questionnaire here. I really tried to make it a searching exposé of the hidden person. However, even with the best will and plenty of time and effort, I could not really transcend the superficial. Marriage is such an obstacle course and the hurdles and ditches along the way differ so much from case to case, that even generalising is to trivialise or to seem to judge. But I have set out some questions that gauge the style of engagement with family life, whether it be long term partnership, married, or married with children. The aim of the quiz is to elicit information that normal conversation and experience in the early stages of a relationship might not draw out. As the quiz is given by a third party, not the loved one or partner, the participant may be more honest and open than otherwise. There will have to be two versions – even handed – one for men to take and one for the ladies. The couple will then be equipped to go forward more informed or split up. The quiz might also be a useful self help tool for those who have been unlucky in love and are trying to find out why or with whom they may find greater success.

Tell me what you think:

For Men

1.   You have been married several years. You have two children. You work hard all week. Your idea of a great way to spend Saturday is:

A) Playing cricket.

B) Watching football.

C) Taking your children to the park.

D) Recovering from Friday night.

E) Shopping.

2.   Your mother tells you that she doesn't like spending time with your wife of 2 years. Your response is:

A) "Tell me more Mum".

B) "Give me a break".

C) "That is disappointing. I would like you to try harder".

D) "Neither do I but I do it anyway".

E) "Let's have lunch and talk about it".

3.   Your eldest child wants you to come to her school music recital but you have an important meeting with clients. You:

A) Make sure your wife attends and takes lots of pictures while you lie to the child saying you were there – at the back.

B) Rush the meeting and arrive late for the music recital.

C) Rearrange the meeting and attend the recital.

D) Try to explain that you cannot be in two places at once and go to the pub instead.

E) Attend the music recital, but dial in to the meeting from the hall.

4. Your wife gets a new short haircut. Your reaction is:

A) Admire it publicly but advise her not to do it again.

B) Love it – it's cool – like Posh Spice.

C) Reluctantly grow to like it – after all she is still the same person.

D) Don't notice.

E) Take her straight out to get extensions.

5. Your 2 year old son is ill – coughing, with a fever - and clearly in distress. Your wife is out with friends. You:

A) Call her from the office and tell her to get home to her responsibilities.

B) Get your mum around to help.

C) Google the symptoms, relieve your son's discomfort with medicine and rock him to sleep on your shoulder.

D) Take him to casualty and call your wife to meet you there.

E) Never hear about it. The nanny is home with him.

6. It is your 10th wedding anniversary. You:

A) Ask your clients around for dinner and hire a caterer.

B) Pick up a curry on the way home.

C) Send flowers (after your children remind you).

D) Forget.

E) Take her shopping.

7. Your wife is thinking of changing jobs/returning to work. Your reaction is:

A) Pleased; as long as it has no impact on you.
B) Diffident – you are not keen on change.
C) Encouraging; new opportunities are exciting.
D) Supportive; the extra cash will be useful.
E) Discouraging; she is not meant to work.

8. Your wife is still 20 pounds heavier than normal, 6 months after the birth of your child. You:

A) Get her a gym membership for her birthday.
B) Enjoy it.
C) Hadn't really noticed. She carries it well.
D) Hadn't really noticed. You are too focussed on the new secretary at the office.
E) Promise her anything she wants at Prada if she loses it.

9. You gain 20 extra pounds after your third child is born. You:

A) Panic, get a physical, join the gym, obsess about losing it.
B) Enjoy it.
C) Cut back on sugar and fat for a while.
D) Blame the baby and your house bound house frau and buy a new car.
E) Get a trainer, some new running gear and sign up for a marathon.

10. Your children and wife want to know where you would like to go for vacation. You:

A) Refuse to take a vacation, blaming work and send them to your mother-in-law for the summer.

B) Don't really care as long as you can relax as a family.

C) Let the family decide, plan and prepare, but enjoy it when the time comes.

D) Insist on going to the same place every year – you know where the pub is and the number of the local babysitter is on speed dial.

E) Treat them to another 6★ luxury hotel with children's club and deluxe spa.

Results.

The man who answers mostly As is struggling with himself as a married man. He always assumed he would get married and he pressured his wife to have children straight away, but the reality is not all that he had imagined. He is never really happy, takes himself very seriously and contrives work, client and club commitments to keep him away from the home. While he loves his wife and children, he cannot enjoy them because his expectations of perfection will not let him relax.

The man who answers mostly Bs is a kind and straight forward bloke. He likes nothing more than a quiet night in watching a football match or episode of Top Gear, with a six-pack and his wife to rub his feet. He is not a chauvinist and helps out where he can around the house, but he is not attentive to detail and can infuriate his family with his boyish ways. Like a child he is easily pleased and is very unassuming. This man doesn't want stress, arguments or criticism.

The man who answers mostly Cs is a rare beast. Chances are he lied on the quiz, but even so, he is a man of his word who really enjoys the company and challenges of marriage and raising a family. He is committed to the idea of a partnership and a union that is more than the sum of the parts. Thorough and self assured, he can be cold and unfeeling at times, but he means well.

The man who answers mostly Ds is a selfish bastard. He cannot bear the thought of being "stuck" with his wife and all her problems. He drinks to excess to forget his choices. He is a victim and cannot take responsibility for his life. He can be dismissive and critical. He is scared and lonely.

The man who answers mostly Es is a fun chap used to fulfilling all his needs and wants. He spoils his loved ones and cherishes them. He is a devoted father, albeit somewhat removed and hopeless when it comes to day to day tasks. What he lacks in wherewithal around the house, he more than makes up for with generosity and playful treats. He is not reckless, but he is easily pleased by material things.

Ask Daniel to answer the questions and see if Polly still wants to marry him after.

Speak soon.

Love to you,

Tx

2 December, 2008

Dear Mum,

I was relieved to hear there are no side effects yet. It's fantastic to hear that you have been allowed afternoons out and about. Such a change from 2 months ago.

We are fine – usual winter sniffles. It is really bitingly cold now – too cold to stand around outside – daytime maximum temperature around 5 or 6 Celsius. We have the school Christmas fair on this Friday. As class rep for the reception year, I have the enviable task of chasing parents of children in that class for contributions towards the cost of food for the fair. It is all rather uncomfortable because at the same time we are asking them to contribute for gifts for the teachers. This comes amidst a recession and just before Christmas, with all its attendant stress and expense. Some parents are incredibly generous in terms of time and financial contributions and they really hold the place together with their energy and kindness. I wish I had the nerve to push the rest of them to do more. I don't blame the people who studiously avoid me on the lookout for donations.

I hope that the fair itself has not taken on more meaning than the occasion. I wonder how it would be to hold a smaller event - say mulled wine and cakes, a card stall where the kids sell their own work, a toy stall where proceeds are donated to charity say, and hold it after or in conjunction with a carol recital or Christmas play. Thereby, getting back to the essence of the season – it is not about wanton consumption or even fund raising. Well actually, for most of the western world it is about exactly that, and stress. But it may be time to take stock of that and say – no – let's

ZOË COPLEY

keep it simple. Jesus was born – hark the herald angels sing - a glass of mulled wine later we can all go home feeling cheery and restored.

I know you are thinking that I should take a step back and not worry about it. I know. I agree. I should. I cannot persuade anyone of my view, though several parents do sympathise, but are happy enough to go with the flow. Ultimately, I will appear to be the mean old Grinch stealing Christmas from the kiddies.

I often wonder what we are telling our children. Pray for the poor people in Africa who have no food, or the victims of an earthquake who lost their homes, but here, go buy yourself 3 hotdogs and some broken toys you will fight with your siblings over later and throw away in three weeks once Santa brings the real thing. Do they know what Christmas means? Could we not collect and donate stuff to hospitals for children who are ill and can't be home for Christmas? Could we do a cooking bee to provide a meal for homeless people or workers who help such people? Could we sell tickets to our school choir concert and raise money for a selected charity? People would say we do enough of that – why can't our own children enjoy a treat for once? You go and run the charity, Tess, seriously. They would be right to say it. I should. I will – next year.

Alright, enough complaints from the sidelines – it is time to just accept that I cannot spoil everyone's fun. If you can't beat 'em, join 'em.

So bring it on then – we need a quiz and games room with huge prizes, donated of course, and a fashion parade where the children model their costume from the various plays and we select the best Joseph and the hippest wise man. We could have a mince pie baking bake–off (no M & S ring-ins) and a Christmas cake competition. The biggest marzipan tree wins! We could sell tree decorations that the kiddies make; we could have a speed tree decorating competition. £5.00 per entry. We could take family portraits with a drummer boy or an elf, a special guest could give away the prizes – maybe a celebrity chef.

The sky is the limit.....

Tx

5 December, 2008

Dear Mum,

I was so happy to speak to you on the phone last night. You sound great – very well and happy.

We are all fine. I came across some interesting research that deals with cancer and hope.

According to David Spiegel MD, Medical Director, Stanford Center for Integrative Medicine and Associate Chair, Psychiatry & Behavioral Sciences, Stanford School of Medicine, the rate of survival and recovery from cancer appears to be higher in patients who live in a state of realistic optimism – not blind optimism – but rather, a realistic acceptance of the situation, together with getting on with their lives. He describes the expression of emotion, the support network, the communication with loved ones and doctors and the facing of fears, as key elements of this improved prognosis and outcome. He runs expressive group therapy programmes, and the Cancer Centre at Stanford[10] also offers writing workshops because:

"Writing is an art form that belongs to every one of you. It is also a powerful tool for healing. Writing is a kind of prayer – a prayer in which you don't ask for anything, except to know your own experience and to make meaning of it.

In the difficult and painful journey through cancer, writing can help. When you write together and share your experiences, it can help you:

---

10. www.stanfordhospital.com

- *Express the complex emotions that come with a diagnosis of cancer*
- *Gain perspective and cope more effectively with life's hardships*
- *Integrate your physical, emotional and spiritual well-being"*

There, that is why I have been writing letters!

Love

Tx

7 December, 2008

Dear Mum,

It is a great relief every time I call to hear that you are so well and that even though the white cells and platelet counts are low you are infection free. How wonderful. And beyond that, you are safely ensconced in the climate controlled comfort of the cancer ward and not sweating it out at home in the Brisbane humidity.

We are all struggling to throw off our spate of colds and viruses. The boys had nasty coughs all last week and now finally Marta and I have also succumbed – we always get sick on the same day with the same illness, caught from the children. I am trying to deny that it may be the flu. I have aching limbs and hot eyes and a headache and sinus pains and an awful phlegmy cough. I do not accept though that it is the flu, as it is years since I last had it and I do believe that denial is the best cure for certain ails.

Also, I hate to accept that my recent whining about the school fair and my lack of gratitude for the opportunity to just have some fun, could be the cause of this malady. You see, I am convinced that when the spirit is depleted all the viruses attack. I have been very well for months – in contrast with recent winters where I have had colds for 4 months running. I was attributing my wellness to my resilient emotional state and my current engagement with life, as evidenced through my new business and general joie de vivre. However, if I am now ill then something has gone astray in my reckoning.

Either I am not spiritually or emotionally as secure as I had thought, my theory is bunkum, I have been denying myself sufficient sleep in my drive to do more, read more and write more or I let my guard down and let the germs in with the negative thoughts and emotions that polluted me last week.

I had a very cranky day on Friday. Serving 300 hot dogs can take a toll. Yes – they did sell like hotcakes. Better. This was the day I began to feel ill. That will bloody well teach me to lose perspective and be such a whingey misery guts. Gratitude is the key to restoring my equilibrium I think. I am grateful for my health generally, and your promising response to the recent treatment. And I am really grateful to Marta for being there to take the little boys while I served hot dogs all afternoon. I fed the masses. I know how the disciples, clearing up after the Sermon on the Mount may have felt.

I return to this letter after over a week to reread my lamentations. What a week. As you know from my calls it was a rotten flu virus and with bronchitis on top and Tommy and Felix concurrently running fevers and coughing all over the house, it has been a blur of five very ill and feverish days. In hindsight I think that the antibiotics I had to virtually beg for were the key to my recovery – but I am grateful indeed for them!

In the middle of the worst of it dear Ingi – one of the mums from school - saved us from a messy debacle by bringing me shopping (toilet paper) and then sending lots of concerned and solicitous texts. Not to mention the wonderful Lizzi, who was on the phone checking in on me as well. We have had the living room taken over as 6 different shops, an underwater world, a boat, a fort and a zoo and a hospital, as all the boys were home to share in the general misery and germ sleepover. Now a full week since the whole achy cycle began, I feel more or less myself again, although it's just turned 7pm and the boys are already asleep; things are not quite normal yet.

I thought Jack would be excited at the idea of returning to school after five days away through my ill health. He said: no, it was all just boring and he only wanted to start his holidays in Ghana. Andrew will be pleased to know he is so excited. I am excited at the thought of the day after we arrive, when I will return after breakfast to lie on the cool sheets of the breezy guest room bed and listen to the birds in the garden. Maybe after a long nap I will emerge to request a trip to a hotel pool for a little relaxing to be followed by juice on the terrace. I will be the lady muck and not lift a finger for three days. Imagine having nothing to do...

I was amused by your dismissive, rather cross tone the other night when I told you about some of my reading in the field of positive psychology. The secrets of happiness and optimism are no mystery to you – oh happy and gleeful one, oh wise and sage guru.

But you see Mum, as I told you, not everyone gets it as you do. You are incredibly well placed – leukaemia aside - to be a happy person. As the research I was referring to suggests, those who are leading a pleasant life doing worthwhile things with which they feel engaged and which involve the engagement of their strengths, tend to be happier than those who are not so connected[11]. Even though we love our crime dramas and chocolate, no one would say that we believe either to be the source of our long term life satisfaction or purpose. As a means of making our lives pleasant they are very effective, but not sufficient for true and sustained fulfilment.

I can see why you might say "what a lot of hooey". But equally, many have neither a pleasant life, nor one in which they feel connected or engaged with their strengths or authentic self, and not for want of trying either.

It may be obvious to some, but it doesn't follow that there is no value in the research or dissemination of the knowledge. The bigger picture is very relevant also. As populations age and the drain on the public purse increases as the health of the elderly becomes a societal

---

11 www.authentichappiness.sas.upenn.edu/

cost, then having a happy and thus healthier, population is in everyone's interest. Helping people to get happy is no small task, given the pulls and drives that seduce and attract them. The cigarettes and alcohol, the club, the team, the job, the bills, the temptation to cut corners, break rules or just be bad. All the false pretences that go with convincing yourself that just one more pound shed or one more drink sipped, will secure that precious happiness you seek... People don't just live like this. Millions live *for* this.

For me, the fact that a whole body of research and endeavour actually scientifically backs up that which you appear to have always known, and as your child I too, by default, have always felt, gives me a great deal of fortitude and reassurance. Instead of feeling isolated and alone in my little bubble of non-consumerist self sufficiency, I now see that millions similarly either share my values or have come to recognise that the road to pleasure and hedonism is a road to nowhere.

As a coach it means that the zeitgeist is ripe for me. I am not a self help nut, per se, but this "happiness" bandwagon has so much in it – at all levels. For me, whichever way one wants to cut the cloth, the client is generally going to be looking to harness his strengths and to maximise his potential and increase his happiness; it's the same dream coat every time.

Turning to a real person for a moment, Claudia came to see me for a chat the other day. I was feeling very ill at the time but was happy for the company and relief from the routine of coughing and sniffling and shivering. She was telling me about a situation she is facing with a man and I truly listened in a deep and nondirective way for a very long time. It was not a coaching conversation as I did little to open her up, or take the discussion anywhere and moreover, we had never agreed it would be. However, unlike normal social chats, I was not very forthcoming or particularly involved. After 90 minutes during which she recited many events of recent weeks she asked whether I agreed that she was handling this fellow superbly. It was the most bizarre thing. If I had been compos mentis at the time I would probably have said "only if your aim is to destroy yourself, go mad or end up depressed; in which case, yes, by all means you are". It has thrown me into a vague wondering as to my value as a friend.

More importantly what is the truth? What is happiness?

Is my subjective view that she is wasting her time and energy on a cad, of any value at all? In spite of hearing more or less this opinion from me a few weeks ago, she is convinced of the merits of her strategy and anything I say to the contrary is either ignored, rationalised, selectively forgotten or compartmentalised. So there is my opinion of what is true and, no doubt, several viable alternate views. But the only one that matters is her truth. Given that she wants this state of affairs to continue, it must have been a very satisfying visit from her perspective. My non-committal response was tantamount to a blessing and endorsement. She has shared and divulged much of herself. She is doing nothing wrong.

So I ask myself, what value did I add? Would a coach have uncovered more? Of course, a question like: "Why do you want someone who you cannot trust?" would open something up, surely. And so that begs the question: is a coach a better friend than a friend? Would I as a coach want my client's happiness more than I seem to want Claudia's? Or is it merely that as a coach I implicitly have the authority or permission I need to be honest? Or is it that as a friend I choose an easy path, the path of least resistance, and rely on coaching now as the means by which to try to be more honest and authentic? Am I qualified, in any case, to have an opinion about what will make her happy in the long run? Is it even about happiness in the first place?

Perhaps this is *her strength* and perhaps her strategy is in fact fulfilling and engaging. Therefore, she has a vocation, which is more than many have. In so following her calling she is busy and thoughtful, investing in herself and in her relationships with others.

She is genuinely committed to her strategy and she believes in what she says. And have I not just projected onto her a desire for fulfilment that may not even be part of her motivations in the first place? While I could not ascribe to her a desire for misery or torment, there are still many other factors that may be driving her.

So even in my flu addled state of hallucinatory cold sweat clarity I saw anew so many things, last night. I lay in bed waiting for sleep to come and it all gelled:

Happiness is incapable of assessment according to objective criteria at all. It is not a "thing", capable of being described and deconstructed, pulled apart and put back together, all its components identified and understood.

It is subjective, and relative, determined by each person according to their individual expectations, experiences, personality and conditioning and only capable of being understood in relation to other states of mind and being. Accordingly, the range of states that can be regarded as ones of happiness are incapable of description or definition. We could all be happy in theory, so long as we say it and seem it.

In assessing what is important or meaningful to someone then, what someone does or thinks can be more important than what they achieve or gain, as it is the journey, not the destination, that contributes most to feelings of engagement and fulfilment. Or put another way, as the old saying goes – it is better to try and fail than never to try at all.

Resilience of spirit is a key virtue and strength: certain behaviour may seem incongruent with happiness, but where the behaviour evidences the fight of the spirit to surmount obstacles or to support the survival of a close held belief, then it seems to bring happiness even though objectively, many indicia of happiness or satisfaction are missing.

Defining happiness is fruitless and pointless. We know it when we feel it though.

There can be happiness without joy or pleasure if there is purpose and engagement.

Then it occurred to me that objective and subjective are too limited as categories of perspectives. One needs further ways to define the relative viewpoints. Maybe "mothectively" – in the eyes of the mother – or "coachectively" – in the eyes of the average coach. Then I realised:

I am the best friend I can be when I am coaching.

Friendship, as I know it, is fundamentally flawed if most of us are not really honest (this will not pertain to you).

Friendship is a key personal relationship or support source proven to be a significant, if not the single biggest, contributor, to a happy state of mind.

If friendship is based in support rather than honest challenge, then the best source of happiness is based in potential lies.

Thus, happiness is purest where disingenuous or where dishonest premises prevail.

Is Happiness then a myth, a mere visage or facade? A fragrance? A car?

Then I fell asleep.

Love you

Tx

7 January, 2008

Dear Mum,

Well our holiday in Ghana was wonderful; restful, busy, restorative. I am completely out of touch with you and I was concerned to hear that you are about to start the third round of chemo.

Dad explained that the biopsy result showed that the leukaemia is back though at a reduced rate – 5-10%. I am sorry to hear it Mummy. This is a setback. We pray that this round will get it all for good and that the drugs are not as harsh on you as they were in September and October.

I am a little lost for words. I have to admit I had begun to blithely believe you were cured.

At least you had a lovely Christmas.

I have no further news apart from our doings in Ghana which you heard on the phone. It was fantastic to have so much space and fresh air and to be surrounded by extended family. It is very heartening I think, especially for Andrew, to be able to dip in and out of this community of loved ones and well wishers, through his frequent visits.

I am looking forward to settling back into work and home life over the next few days. It has been a wonderful long period of time with Andrew. The boys are very relaxed and happy and light-hearted as a result. And yes, Andrew and I enjoyed us all being together as well, before you ask.

The only downside was that I seem to have picked up a tummy bug while in Ghana. This past few days I felt very nauseated as well. I checked my symptoms out online, as all good hypochondriacs now do, and I self diagnosed Irritable Bowel Syndrome. I have all the symptoms. I also have some for stomach ulcer and ovarian cancer. So I saw the doctor today. He is about 19 and looks like a pin-up from a Boy Band – just a little old to be the next star of *High School Musical*. It was a very pleasant experience. We had a great chat about my colon and what might be the problem and I left armed with my little stool sample cup – and scooping spoon in the lid. Tommy liked the look of that and asked whether he could carry it home. I said (fearing long-winded questions, him dropping it in Sainsbury or me having to return, cap in hand, for another one if it rolled under the Number 328 bus) that it had to stay in the bag to keep it really clean. He showed me his hands and insisted they were really clean. Ironic, eh?

My research revealed that 50% of the population suffer from irritable bowels. My earlier letter concerning the suitability of bowel discussions now seems very censorious, indeed. Doctor Doe Eyes said that many of his patients see him for bowel problems, and the research suggested that, even so, bowel concerns are hugely under reported, obviously due to embarrassment. The way the receptionist looks at and refuses to touch the little sample pot when one is submitting the half-full receptacle for analysis, may also contribute to the concealment of this syndrome.

I discovered that the Gut Trust will issue sufferers with a card to entitle the holder to gain access to otherwise unavailable toilets, when one is out and about. Access all areas, big mess coming through! One can join the Gut Trust forum for IBS sufferers and sympathisers and sign a petition for more and better public loos.

Anyway, I expect having said all of that, it is just a passing bug picked up from the water while on holiday. Dr Doe Eyes agrees and suggests more soluble fibre might sort it out.

Much love and best wishes to you and Dad.

Tx

12 January, 2009

Dear Claire,

I am writing from in front of the TV, catching up on the news. How are you? How is Mum? I am taking quite a while to digest the fact that the leukaemia is back and that maybe the reprieve in November was just a short term thing.

I can't say that I am feeling very optimistic anymore. I am compartmentalising this and keeping very busy. I have booked a flight down to Brisbane for mid-March, about which I am very excited and relieved. I cannot wait to see you all. I hope Mum will be alright.

How are you? You are the closest to her, apart from Dad. You see her every day. What do you think will happen?

We are still mulling over the viability of the children and me relocating to Australia later in the year. A move is contingent on many things, but seems feasible. I will keep you informed. After so long here it is hard to make the final decision. Better the devil one knows, I daresay. I have been thinking through a 15 point list to help me make the final decision. Here is what I have come up with:

You know it's time to go when...

1. You cannot for the life of you remember the theme song for *Home and Away*.
2. You feel personally touched and delighted by the "migrating to Australia" help packs online.
3. No one believes you are Australian.
4. Your children are begging to sort their stuff and start packing

and the eldest has written a book called "The family who *mooved* to Brisbane".

5. You have done all the things you came to do.
6. You feel nostalgic about magpies, Fruit Tingles, flat whites and Brisbane newsreaders with 30 year careers.
7. Your mind turns to thoughts of Merve Hughes and Shane Warne affectionately.
8. You realise Roger Federer is more in touch with your homeland than you are.
9. You smile indulgently at young Aussie backpackers on the Piccadilly Line talking too loudly.
10. You start to prefer marmite to vegemite.
11. You go out of your way to buy stashes of Gourmet Traveller magazines, Eucalyptus Honey and Cherry Ripe chocolates to bring back to London after each visit.
12. You get teary when you hear the Qantas song.
13. You begin to feel guilty and resentful that you can't just pop in the car and see your very ill mother, chat with your siblings, and reminisce with your Dad.
14. You convince yourself that your homeland is a magical place where you can feel the hope in the grass and smell the humour in the sky.
15. Help!

I mentioned to Mum that we were considering this move but have not referred to it again. I just want her to focus on getting better and not be worrying about us and our doings. We will sort it out and make the decisions we feel are best for us. Andrew can see the benefits for me and the boys of being close to family and living a more free and outdoors life. As the next couple of months go by we'll have a better idea of when and how to make the move. I am trying to assess the options without letting Mum's situation colour everything. It is pretty hard to do this compartment thing, actually.

Mum herself seems bent on me not coming. She keeps referring to the negatives of life there. The humidity, the problems in the education system, the layoffs in the commodity, mining and related industries. I am not sure whether she is preparing me for some shocks if we come or if she wants to put us off. If what she says is true I will just have to come up with some "decadent" local experiences in the Brisbane environs to compensate for the fact we will no longer be enjoying Britain's perfect weather, resilient economy and far superior education system. Perhaps Bridget can help me draw up a list.

The boys are asking when they can start packing. They are obsessed with planes at the moment. The house is a huge airport. At bed time I have to ask them to come and brush their teeth in the plane bathroom. One positive side effect is that Jack is very happy to do maths homework now that he accepts that pilots do need more than year 2 level addition and subtraction. I am mindful of all the things around the flat that will need attention before we leave. Luckily, I never actioned my plan to put a trampoline in the garden, so no issues with leaving it to be ruined by a rental tenant. I will have to find out how to dissolve superglue from shelves and china and remove a couple of mugs from the cupboard. Having said that, I could leave them and keep the new tenant guessing...

It is going to be thoroughly heartbreaking to throw out so much of the boys' art work – for them. I will hold on to my many "certificates" awarded for being a good mummy. These may come in handy as we adjust to our new life in the antipodes with Daddy's next visit three months away and much blame and recrimination coming my way.

I have been contemplating what I would do if we move to Brisbane. I am keen to be of some help to Mum and Dad, immerse myself in coaching, develop my business ideas and keep up the reading I began last year. I ultimately want to have space – a coaching suite. I have a vision of a Mind Spa at which clients can experience spa style treatments as well as coaching and mind and soul oriented sessions and workshops that will provide a holistic approach to relaxation, rejuvenation and transformation. If I send you my Menu of Services will you look it over? I have also put together a Toolkit for self coaching. This could be part of a small self-help library at the Mind Spa.

I am thinking about my sitcom – if we live in Brisbane there may be no market for my ideas. After all *Neighbours* has been doing "ordinary" for some time. I could still write, though, between visits to the hospital and tuckshop duty and Mind Spa sessions. I hope that you will come and work with me offering counselling services.

Let's speak soon. Love you.

Tx

31 January, 2009

Dear Mum,

Hoping that your white cells are on the mend now and that this week sees an improvement in your neutrophils. We are well. I am writing to say that we are almost definitely going to move to Brisbane before the middle of the year.

I know this is not a huge surprise. I hope you will be home and well for the intervening period and that I can be whatever use to you that you may need when we do come. We are all excited at the prospect; though of course our anticipation is tempered by some regret that we will leave so many wonderful friends and opportunities here. Nevertheless, greener pastures may await, and the chance for what life offers at "home" cannot really be passed up.

I have taken into account your views expressed recently and last year when this notion first came up, given Andrew's extended absences. Rest assured that I am mindful of the impact of long separations on all of us. We have managed pretty well to date. Naturally, 2 or even 3 months without seeing Andrew will be different from 3 week separations, but we are committed to making it work from every perspective. Bring it on.

Also, if it is all too terrible, we can pack up and come back. At least we will know we tried it and the "what if" concerning Australia will be resolved.

I hope this is happy news for you. Please don't make it a source of worry. We are optimistic and happy, yet realistic. Apparently, that is the right combination for weathering storms...

So, in view of my planned visit to see you in March and the

prospect of being a stone's throw away soon after, these letters appear to have run their course. They have certainly helped me. I will no doubt hear from you soon as to what they did for you.

Loads of love

Tx

BOOK TWO
Self Coaching Toolkit

Self Coaching Toolkit

Coaching is a process through which you can clarify your thinking, identify your goals, formulate plans to achieve them and ultimately, transform your reality. Coaching is not rocket science. We all coach our workmates, family, friends and children, often without knowing it. However, when done well – in a focussed, conscious and professional way - coaching has the power to facilitate great transformation and awareness raising. In such cases, the process can indeed seem like art or alchemy.

While coaching is, by definition, best undertaken with a professional coach - listening, questioning and challenging you - with whom you jointly work towards your ambitions, self-coaching is also a useful means of assisting you to develop greater awareness of your current state of mind, where you would like to be, the terrain between those two places, and the nature of any obstacles along the way.

The following self-coaching toolkit offers something for everyone, if not now, perhaps at another time. The value of a toolkit or guide lies in the autonomy and independence with which you can embark on the coaching journey. No appointments, no fees, no guilt when you cancel and go to the pub instead and no person sitting across from you waiting for an answer...

But the coach of a self-coached client may not provide much challenge or objectivity. Sometimes, such a coach may collude with you or even undermine you.

Nevertheless, self coaching remains a viable, valid and sustainable means of taking stock of where you are, clarifying your aspirations and challenging your perceptions and mindsets.

This toolkit is divided into four parts:

241

Stocktake - exercises that require you to pause and consider your life at the moment.

The Dream – questions and prompts that encourage you to look a little deeper into yourself with a view to better understanding what motivates and drives you; what your aspirations and visions are for yourself.

"Get out of your way" – challenges that help you to identify and own up to the internal and self imposed obstacles that may impede change or growth.

The Way – suggestions that help you find and stay on the path towards your Dream. The following diagram illustrates the process:

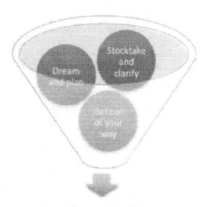

Transform and grow

The tools and exercises that follow are practical and working space has been provided for your use. Take your time and enjoy the process.

Stocktake - Exercise 1[12]

Before you embark on a coaching journey or begin planning for change, it may be useful to consider more carefully the areas of your life in which you feel more challenged or less satisfied.

Below is a list of eight different aspects of your life. This is not an exhaustive list. Feel free to add or remove categories. The aim of this exercise is to assess your current feelings in relation to each category. Give each aspect a score from 0–10 with 10 representing the highest level of satisfaction and 0 representing virtually no satisfaction with the category in question.

1. Finances
2. Social/Friends
3. Work/Career
4. Leisure Pursuits
5. Health/Fitness
6. Spiritual/Religious
7. Partner
8. Family

Were there any surprises?

---

12 A similar model - described as "The Wheel of Life" by Whitworth, Kimsey-House, K and H, and Sandal in Co-active Coaching 2007, p 222ff, is a widely used coaching tool, aimed at helping clients identify their values and areas in which they are living in accordance with them or otherwise. I make no claim to have developed this tool.

Now that you have scored these key categories, give each one a further score to reflect each of the following:

a) the satisfaction level you perceive your closest friends and family would regard you as having in each category; and
b) your ideal level of satisfaction for each category.

Are there any areas in which you are highly satisfied?

Are there any which others would have a different view from that which you hold about your level of satisfaction?

Are you noticing anything in particular?
E.g. You are good at portraying certain attributes to loved ones but secretly feel quite differently or that your ideal satisfaction levels tally closely with other's perception of you.

This exercise is intended to raise your awareness about:

a) what is going well right now;

b) areas in which you feel less satisfaction, but ideally would like to feel more satisfied;

c) any mismatch or disparity between what you feel is highly satisfying and what others might say;

d) any relationships between what you regard as 'ideal' and what you perceive others expect of you;

e) any actions you might take to alter your satisfaction levels; and

f) the extent to which you feel able to influence your level of satisfaction in any area.

Record here anything that you are noticing.

On what would you like to focus in order to increase your actual satisfaction level now?

How realistic is it to attempt that?

E.g. say the exercise has revealed that you would like to go to the gym more often. Can you accommodate this wish given time constraints or pressure that may result on areas with which you are already satisfied?

Are you thoroughly confused?

Have you decided after doing the exercise that you are jolly happy after all?

If so – well done!

If not – keep reading. Perhaps try Stocktake Exercise 2.

Stocktake – Exercise 2

If you:

a) Hate questionnaires and quizzes;

b) Refuse to write down your feelings and thoughts;

c) Resent being held accountable;

d) Got nothing out of Exercise 1; or

e) Tend to buck the system, pooh–pooh authority and disdain order and structure;

then this exercise may be useful for you.

Describe in as few words as possible how you feel about your life.

What do you have or what do you do that gives you happiness?

List at least two things you do not enjoy or which you like least right now.

List at least two things you would like more of or to do more often.

If the writing is getting you down, why don't you try to draw the feeling you have about your life right now?

If you could, what would the picture show?

Pictures paint a thousand words... come on.

Ok, fine. Can you describe this feeling in terms of a film (or a book) you are familiar with?

Here are some ideas to help you:

Forrest Gump (you never know what you will get)
The Godfather (your family runs your life and you feel death is imminent)
27 Dresses (always the bridesmaid never the bride)
Wall Street (greed is good)
The Man who Knew too Much (busybody gets comeuppance)
Fight Club (weird hobbies keeping you away from real world)
Clueless (at any level)
Gladiator (warrior, hero, fighter, death defying maverick – to a point)
Knocked up (say no more)

Unforgiven (speaks for itself)
The Great Escape (so now what?)
The Mirror Cracked (time for a new look)
Enemy of the State (on the run, alone)
Sex and the City (it's all about the shopping and the men)
The Good Girl (no fun)
Alice in Wonderland (no idea where you are)
Le Divorce (it sounds better in French)
Liar Liar (you or someone you know)
The Mummy (not yet dead)
An Inconvenient Truth (so what are your options)
A Bug's Life (oohhhh...)
Hair (really?)
Friends with Money (must you keep up?)

So? Name a film or book:

Ok. Hopefully you now have a better handle on how you feel.

Stocktake - Exercise 3

This exercise may be helpful if you already know exactly where you are and what areas you would like to focus on, or if having completed Stocktake Exercises 1 and/or 2 you feel that you have identified areas of concern or facets of your life that you would like to clarify or manage better. Stocktake – Exercise 3 focuses on how to rediscover the good things, learning from the past so as to enhance our sense of congruity and authenticity. When our actions are in keeping with our intrinsic self, we feel things are right or satisfying.

In Stocktake – Exercise 1 we focussed on our satisfaction with our lives right now. In Stocktake - Exercise 2 we tried to sum up our overall feeling about our situation and identified what is currently making us happy or less than happy. Let us now turn to what historically has gone well.

Consider times when you have felt happy and unburdened, free and easy.

Now think back to times when those feelings have not been accompanied by a lot of alcohol or a win at the track.

Now reflect on what conditions were present at those times of unburdened satisfaction or "flow"[13].

---

13   For more context around what is meant by "flow" see Tim Gallwey's website www.theinnergame.com and his book The Inner Game of Tennis (1975). Also see Mihaly Csikszentmihalyi – "flow" happens when we become so absorbed in an activity that we lose ourselves and our sense of time is altered: www.centreforconfidence.co.uk

E.g. You were with friends, relaxing.
You were achieving well at work.
You were helping others.
You were absorbed with an interest.

Now look more deeply at that experience and what else was happening in your life at that time.
E.g. Were you in a relationship? What was happening at work? What was happening at home? Where were you physically located?

What else do you remember? What could you see, smell, touch, hear?

Were any other feelings present apart from the free and happy ones? E.g. were you eager, anxious, tired, stressed, under pressure, feeling obligated, guilty or sad?

Now consider whether the conditions, context and surrounding events have any continuing relevance for you?

Are the "good times" you identified still accessible? Do you want them to be? How can you ensure they stay where you want them to be?

The Dream

Based on the Stocktake exercises you may have identified areas or topics with which you are feeling stuck or dissatisfied. You may also be clearer as to the areas in which things are going well. At this point in time you may wish to pause and reflect on how you would like to proceed. You may feel that you are ready to take the learning from the Stocktake and work on increasing the things that are going well, that have made you happy or that give you most satisfaction. You may know exactly how to do this.

What next?

One way forward is to look at the bigger picture.

This section invites you to consider the wider perspective. Suspend reality and explore your hopes and aspirations, your plans or desires. Take time to reflect on where you want to be and what you want to achieve[14]. What is your Dream?

The Dream may be very vague, very all encompassing or very long-term. It may involve a series of small desires. Whatever form it takes, take the time now to reflect on it.

Jot down some of your thoughts here.

---

14 While I would hate to suggest any judgement or condemnation of another's dream, I would suggest that only legal and vaguely ethical yearning should be part of this exercise. If the dream is to make squillions of pounds through VAT fraud it might be opportune to find a new dream...

Also, let's keep it clean. Oh and no harming self or others.

You may already know your Dream. You may be living it right now (in which case – shut this book and get on with it), or feel that it is close. You may need to reconnect with your innermost hopes. You may need to revisit goals set in the past with which you no longer identify.

Depending on how you feel about the Dream, whether indeed you have one, the following exercises may help.

What is the Dream?

Which of the following categories do you feel you are in?

No Dream

1. There is no Dream, never has been, never will be.
2. There once was a Dream, I forget when or what it was.
3. There was a Dream but it's silly and childish.
4. There is no Dream – I would like to have one.

A Dream of sorts

5. There is a Dream but it will only ever be that.
6. There is a Dream but it is not really me anymore.
7. There is a Dream - I am not sure about it though.
8. There is a Dream – I hold it dear and want to fulfil it.

A real and clear Dream

9. There is a Dream and it is clear and meaningful.
10. There is a Dream and I am on my way to fulfilling it.
11. There is a Dream and it has been fulfilled.

In relation to each case above, or in the event that a further category applies better to you, there follow a number of questions. I have set these out in a table for ease of reference. Feel free to jot down your thoughts in the table.

There is:	So...	Think about:	Then write down:
No Dream...	skip this entirely or play along.	A blue and cloudless sky. Daydream for a few minutes – let your mind wander, imagine you are granted three magic wishes...	The three wishes...
A Dream of sorts...	reflect on this Dream and its current relevance to you.	The elements that are still meaningful or dear to you.	What came to mind and what the Dream now looks like.
A real Dream	Identify the aspects of this that are already partially or totally fulfilled.	What else you need to do to fulfil the dream, or create a new Dream.	What remains to be done.
Just confusion e.g. I am not able to dream or do Blue Sky thinking.	Consider using a metaphor that works for you. e.g. nuts and bolts, bare bones or back to basics,	What do I want today, next week, next year...?	What I want...

With the outcomes from the above table in mind, how do you feel now?

E.g. lighter, happier, worried, oppressed, confused, anxious, self absorbed, bored.

Still no Dream?

If you have no Dream, don't worry. Maybe something will coalesce in your subconscious mind. Close this book and go and do something else.

It is possible that you are someone who does not have dreams and never will – in which case, apologies for wasting your time.

It could be that you need to speak with someone to help unlock your thinking. Is there a friend or trusted colleague or animal you could confide in and bounce ideas around with?

A Dream is emerging?

Do something to make that dream a living part of you. Tell someone. Draw it, record it in some way. Keep it somewhere safe, but within reach. Give it some air and sun to help it grow and blossom.

There is a clear dream

Share it or savour it. Revel in it. Embrace it.

Potential problems

Sometimes this sort of exercise creates confusion, or even frustration and irritation.

It's all very well to dream, you may say, but what about the here and now, the reality? You may be thinking: dreams won't get the ironing done or find me a job; a dream will not get my son through his A levels or cure my Dad of cancer.

Indeed. But while you were dreaming did you feel different; lighter, happier, albeit momentarily?

Really? Ok. Sometimes the concerns of daily life and the stress of family, work and relationships can weigh us down and impede us from accessing the part of our minds that allow us to hope and aspire.

Is something preventing you from formulating a Dream or embracing the idea that you can have one? If so, what is it?

Can you just let go of that for a moment?

Try not to dwell on these concerns. If something is crystallising, then savour it.

Be with and embrace a chance, a vision or hope, no matter how far-fetched or out of reach it may seem. Maybe the Dream that has emerged seems too pedestrian or banal. Perhaps you feel disappointed that you want so little or conversely, overwhelmed by the extent of your unsatisfied yearnings for more. In any case, try to accept what has emerged. This process has unlocked some aspiration. Look on it as the first step on a path towards a future that you want for yourself. Be with this vision for a time and see what happens.

"Get out of your way"

In the exercises that follow I invite you to take a good look at the ideas and images, expectations and judgements that get in your way. You may have encountered some of these during the earlier exercises; if not consciously, certainly at an unconscious level. It is virtually impossible to enter into any sort of thinking or reflecting exercise, without our deeply held or innate beliefs informing how we process the question and reach our answers.

Many of these beliefs or what I shall call, self-images and self-judgements, can be enabling and powerful tools. For example, the belief that I am a good cook, that I enjoy making new friends, that I am thorough and meticulous at my work.

Jot down a few of your positive self-beliefs here:

(Feel free to use extra paper if you need to.)

At the same time, our thoughts and ideas can also be influenced in a less positive way. I may believe that I cannot run fast, that I am pedantic or narrow minded. Whether or not these beliefs have a foundation in truth or are objectively accurate is not the issue. The fact is that whatever the nature or substance of the belief or judgement, if its impact is to limit, control or disparage, then it is worth challenging or testing.

Accordingly, this stage of the Toolkit is designed to test, and where appropriate, to undermine, the self-limiting beliefs and philosophies that get in the way of our happiness, limit our potential and prevent us from fulfilling our dreams.

There are many ways in which we get in our own way. The following is a list of just some of the things we say to ourselves – often without conscious thought or awareness. As you read the list, note any recent examples of where you may have used one of these devices to hold yourself back, talk yourself down or stop yourself from doing something:

I could not do...

I am too fat/plain/old/stupid/inexperienced/to do...

No one would be interested in what I think.

I always mess this up.

I never know what to do.

I am such a sap.

I hate the way I...

If only I had x I could do y.

I made so many mistakes in the past, it is too late for me...

I couldn't make a difference.

What is the point.

Can you think of any other beliefs you express about yourself that are similarly limiting?

Sometimes the belief is less about our abilities or aptitudes, and more about opportunities or the past. Such beliefs tend to go hand in hand with a sense that we are powerless or ineffectual. They can amount to a statement of victimhood.

E.g.

I have no idea what to do in relationships; I had no positive role models growing up.

I will probably be a crap parent – mine were shockers.

Men always dump me. There is something wrong with me.

Everyone in my family was good at x, except me.

Why do these things always happen to me?

I could go on for pages with lists of examples of ways in which we restrict ourselves, excuse our failings and hold ourselves back. The lesson for us is to notice when we do it and why we do it.

Is it because we believe the statement, because we think people around us believe it of us, or because it's what someone once said so we have internalised it and convinced ourselves it must be true without ever questioning it?

Or indeed, perhaps, to date, the statement has been true.

We need to consider one further way in which beliefs can get in our way. While in many cases the thing that holds us back is easily identified as a belief about ourselves, others or our situation, it is also often true that the fundamental belief is deeply buried or concealed beneath layers of negative feelings such as guilt or discomfort, remorse or grief. It may be that we hardly notice that we are limiting our options or restricting our perception of our opportunities, skills or talents because we operate at a level at which all we notice are habitual ways of behaving coupled with feelings of negativity.

These situations are often very complex and the underlying

emotions and rationalisations are seemingly impenetrable. We feel bad when we overindulge. We feel guilty when we arrange time away from our families. We regret that we are not better at making friends. The list goes on. We are so used to living with these feelings of guilt or ill-ease that we have come to believe that this is just how things are. We do not realise that it might be possible to feel any other way.

Sometimes, we are so reluctant to even feel guilt, that we construct yet another layer of complexity. When a little feeling of self-loathing starts to creep in we stop it in its tracks and replace it automatically with a projected resentment or loathing about the source of the guilt. There are many very qualified counsellors, psychologists and psychotherapists who could better explain this process than I can here. Suffice to say, we can all think of times when we have been almost irrationally and inexplicably cross about something or someone. I am not referring to occasions where we were wronged or cheated and feelings of anger were a natural response, objectively appropriate. Rather, I mean situations where by any objective standard we overreact or even become upset with very little or no provocation, even pre-emptively.

If we could break down all the guilt and negative emotion so that we could identify the underlying beliefs and the situations in which the belief triggers the guilt, we might be able to change, let go, get out of our way.

Over to you.

List as many of the circumstances in which you feel bad, guilty or self loathing as you can:

Here are some examples to get you thinking:
    Not calling home to check on the children during the day.

Drinking too much on the weekend.
Skipping the gym/run.
Criticising a friend or colleague.
Resenting a partner's presence/ideas.
Wasting time.
Wanting more.

What, if anything, do you notice about the things that make you feel guilty?

Can you think of any times when you felt incredibly resentful or angry, out of proportion to the provocation, or in the absence of provocation?

Ok. It is quite confronting, eh?

Now the question becomes – what underlies the guilt, the anger or the self-loathing?

This may be really obvious, now that you have focussed on the negative feeling. Or it may be very difficult to see the wood for the trees.

Given that only you can answer this question, I would challenge you to do so now. I hasten to add that this is not an easy exercise to do on your own. You may want to ask a trusted friend to help you to delve deeper into the feelings to get to their root and source.

Here is a sample: Why do you feel upset, even guilty, if you don't have a great day with your children? What is the belief that underpins the guilt? Is it that you believe your family should be a source of joy all the time? Is it that you believe good parents never feel bored or frustrated around their children? Is it that you had an expectation that parenting would be fulfilling and not finding it so all the time leaves you feeling that you have made bad choices?

Use this space to record anything you discover.

Right. You have some choices now. The above exercises helped you to isolate beliefs, assumptions and judgements that may get in your way. Now what?

Here are some options:

1. Let go of the belief or judgement – just ignore it, deny it and tell it to go take a running jump.
2. Ask yourself what is the positive intent behind that belief or judgement.
3. Look more closely at the belief and question why it is there. Understand where it comes from and see if there is a positive way to recast it.
4. Trump the belief with an alternative, enabling, empowering statement and see how that feels.
5. Embark on a process of slowing down the inner voices and beliefs through some mindfulness (meditation) training, so as to accept and recognise these thoughts as they happen. Acknowledge the thought; then let it go right by you. It is not you, it is not who you are, it is just a thought.

Let's give it a go:

Belief	Positive intent	Restatement in positive terms	Alternative belief	Further challenge
I am a terrible parent.	I want to be a good parent.	While I lack confidence in myself I really want to parent well.	I can be a great parent – this is really important to me.	What is a "good parent"?

I am too old to change career.	A fresh start is worth considering.	I feel that time is not on my side but I have loads of experience and gravitas.	I can try something new – nothing is new for long and I have been through enough to be able to trust my instincts.	Do you need to change at all? Do you need to see it as a change?
I am destined to have a go nowhere mediocre job.	I would like to feel motivated and excited at work.	I have been cruising and it's time to make a change.	I have the energy and desire to control what I do and where I work.	What is a "go-nowhere mediocre job"?

Now *you* try to do this in relation to some of your self-limiting beliefs. Don't choose all the easy ones that you only say in the hope of appearing modest and likeable. Go for something ingrained and really negative.

Belief	Positive intent	Restatement in positive terms	Alternative belief	Further challenge

What did you notice?

Did it get easier as you went on?

Do you still hold the original beliefs?

Ok, you, again. Look, it's not a magic trick. But it is a useful way of challenging and training yourself to be more positive and to believe in the possibilities. Try to make time to take stock of a situation and apply the four new ways of looking at it or yourself as you did when you filled out the table above. After a while it will become second nature to start to look for the positive spin, the flipside of the coin, the silver lining.

Roles we play

In addition to recognising when we are being our own worst enemy through the self-limiting beliefs and judgements we apply, it is useful to discover how our judgement of situations and of others can also limit us. Our assumptions can get us off the hook. We can shirk responsibility, shy away from change or step in to save the day. We can be the victim, the martyr, the knight in shining armour.

By assuming certain roles we can limit our options and stifle our creativity. Some roles constitute a projection of a self belief that drives us to habitually behave in ways that allow others to treat us poorly, take us for granted or disregard our authentic needs.

Here are some examples of roles that we might assume:
Mother and protector.
All conquering hero.
Helpless child.
Wise one.
Great big drip/Big girl's blouse.
Goody two-shoes.

Rebel/ Party animal.

Boss.

Victim.

Policeman.

You may be thinking that none of those roles involve limiting beliefs; they are merely personality or character traits, preferred ways of operating. Sometimes we may even feel we are playing to our strengths.

That is certainly true to some extent and I am not suggesting that we should stop being who we are or that just because we are looking at ourselves, we should throw the baby out with the bathwater.

Nevertheless, it is still true that we do not need to habitually take on a particular role. Sometimes we resent the person with whom we are involved when we step into the role in question. Sometimes we just feel put upon or taken for granted, hemmed in or stifled because we feel that we have no choice but to take on the particular role.

On other occasions we fulfil certain roles out of self interested desires for recognition, praise or attention. There is nothing intrinsically wrong with that, so long as it accords with our real goals and outcomes. Is it in alignment with our sense of who we are, where we are going, or our Dream?

For example: I know that I want to make more time for myself. I am feeling very tired and run down. My social life is too demanding. My friends have come to expect me to party every week. I want to find a new hobby or interest that enables me to enjoy solitude and spend more time at home.

Would it be congruent then, to continue to play the role of party animal, or the wise man taking calls from friends looking for solutions to their problems?

What if I want to take control of my life and stop feeling

powerless in the face of a strong parent or partner? Would continuing to play a helpless child be productive?

The inquiry then is this:

> Do I tend to assume certain roles?
> Do these roles fulfil my bigger picture objectives or get in my way?
> Am I limiting myself by taking on these roles?

Pause to work through these questions now:

Note that even what may seem to be a powerful, important or nurturing role, may be out of synch with who you are or what you have defined as your Dream or goals.

Raising these issues necessarily involves a consideration of how a change of approach on your part may impact the other players in your life.

- Will your wife be pleased if you stop being the all conquering hero?
- Will your mother mind if you grow up and make your own choices?
- Will your children mind if you are less of a Policeman?
- Will your colleagues be lost if you stop taking charge of every situation?

Given that change is not easy, what could you do to help the people around you accommodate your desires to be more true to yourself?

Recap

So where are we?

We have highlighted the areas in which we feel good, even fulfilled. We have identified where we would like to put some thought and energy with a view to making some changes. We have started to articulate the bigger picture and to focus on our longer term aspirations as to where we want to go and what we really want to achieve with our lives. Hopefully the aspirations and goals accord in some way with the values that we felt we needed to honour more in the Stocktake process.

Finally, we have gained some insight into ways in which we may sabotage our process and progress; by listening to self-limiting critical inner voices and taking on roles that restrict us.

Now we should tie all of this together with a review of some of the key strengths or virtues you feel you embody and the extent to which you are making the most of these – using these in your day to day life.

Research suggests that where you use and nurture your strengths you achieve a more authentic and meaningful existence. While this may never have been an articulated goal, it cannot but help in achieving what are your explicit goals and Dreams set out above. Moreover, if you are acting more congruently, in a way more in keeping with who you are and where you excel then it would seem that your ability to feel some of those delightful periods of flow and engagement should increase.

I cannot do better than refer you to the work of the team at UPENN – Authentic Happiness for more. I recommend you take the Strengths Survey provided on the website and peruse the material at your leisure[15].

---

15 www.authentichappiness.sas.upenn.edu

Great stuff, eh?

What else? Oh yes –

The Way

There are thousands of books available to coach you through the next stages. I had thought when I began to write this Toolkit that I too would be thorough and fulsome and set out a set of guidelines or suggestions for the Way itself. The "journey", as it were. How to coach yourself though various issues and using the learning from the above exercises I would turn you out a changed person after reading this guide.

I am no longer inclined to that view. Here is why:

I cannot coach you with a book. You are a unique and fascinating individual and your concerns and ideas and thoughts, even the self-limiting ones that have survived (there will be some, even many) will create such an intricate and elaborate kaleidoscope of reactions and perceptions that attempting to set out the next steps, the "how" to make the change and stick to it seems utterly contrived and presumptuous. I have no idea what you are thinking right now. Let's face it, you may not either. I had no idea at the outset and ploughed in anyway, but I feel that in my ideal state as a "less is more" coach, to start directing you further at this point would be very misconceived.

If I were to start telling you what to do next, I am at a loss as to how I could accommodate all readers? Some of you may think this is a pile of old cobblers. If you are my mum you will think it is a load of "hooey". If you are my brother you will be thinking what a lot of self indulgent claptrap. Others may think that I made a few good points but overall it was a waste of time. One or two may feel that this has helped unlock some doors into their mind space and freed up their thinking.

But in terms of taking that thinking forward, I think it's over to you now...

I concede that I am taking the easy way out here. I have led you on a merry dance and now abandoned you to find your own way home. I will not hide the fact that more savvy coaches or writers would be penning the next chapter right now. For me, I sense that the next stage is really a complex flowchart representing the many decision trees that now follow. There are so many unknowns and blank spaces on that tree though, especially with a hypothetical unseen client – such as you - dear reader, that to prescribe the next steps, would be reductive, even unhelpful.

You know what to do next.

Yes you do.

You are still here?

Oh, alright. But only a few tips – just little suggestions. You *do* know what to do next.

You can do any or all of the following:

a) Using the learning from the above exercises, continue to keep a record or journal of what you value, dream and believe about yourself until it becomes clear what you want to be doing next and how to start doing it.

b) Ask yourself lots of open questions that force you to look at things more broadly and from new perspectives.

c) When you think you are clear about something check in with a challenging question.

d) Try to think of new ideas or new approaches to problems by stepping in and out of different roles or characters – perhaps ones you admire in others or that you feel might offer a fresh or valuable perspective.

e) When you feel disconnected or frustrated about something that has happened or may happen, pause and look within yourself for the source of that disconnection. Accept it, don't try to deny it or gloss over it, look for whether that feeling is trying to tell you something.

f) Learn to meditate to become more aware of the processes that are going on within you.

g) Hire a coach to help take this process further.

BOOK THREE
Games

Coaching Word Search

A	F	D	A	N	C	E	F	A	T	O	G	E	C
A	N	G	E	R	L	M	E	I	I	J	D	T	L
R	U	I	N	A	A	E	C	Q	S	B	I	P	A
U	P	O	O	S	I	R	S	L	S	M	C	E	R
O	I	L	Y	P	N	G	N	R	U	O	A	R	I
N	L	P	H	I	E	E	O	W	E	I	U	M	F
O	M	A	E	R	D	X	C	K	S	C	Z	I	Y
H	N	E	M	E	R	O	L	A	G	C	P	T	R
E	X	P	E	N	S	I	V	E	G	U	D	O	D
E	N	I	L	Y	R	R	O	W	O	G	I	K	H
A	G	O	G	Y	R	T	Y	T	I	R	A	L	C
C	H	A	L	L	E	N	G	E	X	P	L	B	Z

Riddles

Q. What do you get if you cross a lawyer with a coach?
A. A detail oriented know-it-all who charges too much for nodding sagely.

Alright, you make some up, smarty pants!

Crossword

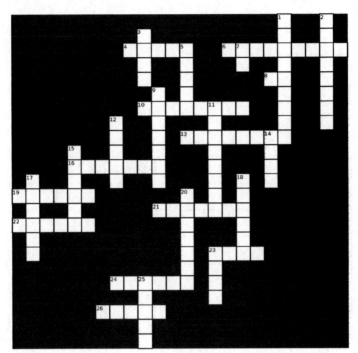

Across

4   Salty water
6   Attention, hearing
8   I'm OK, You're…
10 Strong, mighty
13 Animal with a trunk
16 Absence of sound
19 Biscuit
21 Brand of shoe
22 Caffeinated beverage
23 Resonate, makes sense
24 Elegant dance
26 Communication device

Down

1   Small group discussion
2   Agreement
3   Expression of emotion
5   Area
7   Ego
9   Process of moving
11 Criticism
12 Emotion
14 Serious or intense student
15 Hope
17 Word for respect
18 Idea about the future
20 Bond or connection
23 Plot of earth
25 Day time meal

BOOK FOUR

Spring to Mind Coaching Mind Spa

Ethos

At Spring to Mind Coaching we value space and time to reflect and think. We call this "mind space". We believe that when we harness and maximise the ideas and inspiration that emerge from our mind space we can embark on transformational journeys.

Coaching is but one facet of what a Spring to Mind – Mind Spa offers you.

Whatever your motivation, Spring to Mind can help you clarify your thinking, rediscover your equilibrium, nurture your dreams, connect with your true self.

Our unique services incorporate a blend of coaching, training, treatment and support group. Leave your worries at the door and move into a new mind space.

Rejuvenate and refresh.

Spring to life. Spring into action. Find your inner spring.

Spring to Mind – Mind Spa is an Urban Retreat, divided into a number of spaces where clients can focus on their particular needs.

Spring Body Space

As well as a state of the art Gym and swimming pool with specially designed lighting that enhances you, rather than exposes you, and mirrors and rest areas that motivate you to workout, Mind Spa Spring Body Space offers a range of active classes and group fitness sessions intended to put the fun back into exercise.

For the Uber Fit:

High Kicks and High Jinks – a high energy aerobic workout for the super fit. Bored with stepping up and pulsing it out? Then this is the class for you. Our instructor, Kevin, guarantees no two routines are alike. Not only your body, but also your mind and memory, will be stretched as you pirouette, can-can and cartwheel your way around the studio. (Knee pads optional).

Commando Cruising – ex-marine, Charlie, will get those abs tight and those buns light with this intense adventure based workout. Test your ingenuity, mettle and inner thighs on our bespoke obstacle course.

Pushover – bring out the child in you with rough play and rumpus style work out techniques. Devised by 8 year olds, Pushover will have you roaring with laughter as you elude the tickling probes, escape the water bombs and duck for cover as the pillow fights erupt.

We know all too well that not everyone has coordinating gym kit, a desire for a six pack or a pair of clean trainers. Some of our clients have not been inside a gym for some time. We respect and cater to that. We welcome all ability, interest and fitness levels. We applaud effort over execution and substance over style. So pull on the old Dunlop Volley sandshoes, slip on an oversized t-shirt and dust off the skipping ropes and elastics that kept you fit in 1982.

We have a special range of classes of a shorter duration to ease you back into it. These are designed for all self respecting newbies, wanna-bes and pudgees.

Unco Yoga – a gentle blend of sun salutes and toe touching. You've never seen a downward dog like this before!

Balance – walk straight, stand tall and look your reflection in the eye, all while balancing a book of your choice on your head.

Bo-i-nngg – set to the upbeat and irresistible melodies of the Stock Aitken and Waterman stable of stars, this class has you bouncing (literally, on our flouro hop balls) around our Sunshine Studio. When the going gets tough on the old thighs, you bounce right over to the super large trampolines and rediscover your youth. (Maximum weight restrictions apply.)

Being a holistic organisation we recognise that some of our clients prefer to stay fit using a range of techniques not typically found under one roof. Accordingly, we offer special experiences in the Spring Body Space.

For our Ice Queen clients there is the Frisson Space with 20 metre high ice wall, mini ice rink and cold room (excellent for taking your mind off your worries and burning fat).

For the Water Nymphs we cater to both active and sedentary preferences in our Luxury Lagoon Space. Consider:

Water Ballet (tutus provided).

Synchronised Swimming (nose clips available from the Pool Boy).

Deep Immersion Pool – an abyssal experience in a 15 metre deep diving pool. The challenge lies in resisting the ebbs and flows of the random currents and riptides. (Life jackets available on request.)

Alpha Aqua Avalanche - an intense and invigorating experience in which industrial strength hoses batter and blast you through three stages – the hit and miss, the power shower and the water slide to freedom.

Treatments

Naturally, being a spa, we offer traditional treatments such as massage, facials, manicures and body wraps.

Some of our special treatments in the Pamper Space include:

Total Makeover packages – hair, teeth, attitude, body image and mindset. *Hot Stone Therapy* – a visualisation therapy – who would you like to pelt hot stones at?

Lavage and Lose it – a bespoke cellulite buster.

Coaching

In the Learning Space we offer workshops and seminars to help you sort out your ideas and priorities. A sample include:

Meditation and Mindfulness – learn to slow down and live in the moment.

Making time for me – harness your selfish whims and give them purposeful life.

Rediscover your Inner Child – using a combination of toilet humour, play-dough and dressing up, discover a simpler way of seeing things.

Find your Voice – role play, ad libbing and free association.

Now say it and Mean it – develop subtle and persuasive assertiveness techniques (very useful within marriages).

The Visible Woman – learn ways of being more noticeable and increasing your impact.

Aqua Therapy – a range of water based treatments achieving several benefits including cleansing the mind of negativity, washing away the proverbial crap dumped at your door, sifting through the detritus and debris washed up on the shore of one's life, going with the flow, riding the current and no longer fighting the tide.

Clear Out and Declutter – find out what makes you a hoarder – learn how to let go of *stuff* yet retain control.

Well-Being

In the Emotion Space we offer suites dedicated to specific needs. For expressing Anger try the Belt it and Bash it Room. For frustration and desperation the Steam and Scream Room is a favourite (it also fights wrinkles, cellulite and fluid retention and surveys show that a 3 minute scream session and a cool glass of water achieves the same results as 20 minutes on the treadmill and a full body massage). The Tears on my Pillow Room is a zen hideaway where you can relax and let it all out, knowing you will leave intact after a mini-facial and restorative head massage.

We also have a Gratitude Room, a Guilt-Free Room, a cyber cafe and juice bar, with complimentary salads, a wine bar specialising in wines from the Antipodes, and a state of the art, sustainable crèche.

Coming Soon

Spring to Mind has plans to open several more branches in the near future.

Check our website for details of opening promotions at Spring to Mind – Mind Spa's:

Countryside - a rural idyll featuring accommodation, alfresco treatments and connection with mother earth.

Seaside - windswept and active detoxification awaits. Blow out the cobwebs and wash in a new you.

Hilltop - scale new summits and feel your soul take flight while meditating amidst the majesty of the mountains.

Resources

Faber, Adele & Mazlish, Elaine, 2001; *How to Talk So Kids Will Listen and Listen So Kids Will Talk,* Piccadilly Press Ltd.

Kimsey-House, Henry; Kimsey-House, Karen; Sandah, Phil; Whitworth, Laura; 2007 (2nd ed); *Co-active Coaching: New Skills for Coaching People Toward Success in Work and Life,* Davies Black Publishing.

Napthali, Sarah, 2003; *Buddhism for Mothers: A Calm Approach to Caring for Yourself and Your Children,* Allen & Unwin.

Seligman, Martin E.P., 2002; *Authentic Happiness,* Simon and Schuster

Australian Department of Immigration and Citizenship - www.immi.gov.au

Authentic Happiness - www.authentichappiness.sas.upenn.edu

Coaching Development - www.coachingdevelopment.com

Dr Phil – www.drphil.com

International Coach Federation – www.coachfederation.org

International Positive Psychology Association (IPPA) - www.ippanetwork.org

Kübler-Ross Grief Cycle – changingminds.org

Play on Words Communication Coaching for Children - www.play-on-words.co.uk

Rheingold – www.rheingold-online.de

Spring to Mind Coaching - www.spring-to-mind.co.uk

Stanford Integrative Health - www.stanfordhospital.com

Tim Gallwey - www.theinnergame.com

BBC - news.bbc.co.uk/1/hi/programmes/happiness_formula

NCIS - www.cbs.com/primetime/ncis/

The West Wing - www.westwingepguide.com

Seven Up - en.wikipedia.org/wiki/Seven_Up!

Leaukeamia

Acute Myeloid leukaemia - *en.wikipedia.org/wiki/Acute_myeloid_leukemia*

Cancer Research UK - www.cancerresearchuk.org

Leukeamia Research Fund - www.lrf.org.uk

Macmillan Cancer Support - www.macmillan.org.uk

National Cancer Institute – www.cancer.gov

Acknowledgements

To Mum and Dad, for giving me such a wonderful and happy beginning and for always being there.

To Francis, for all of your love, support and encouragement and for your belief in my capacity to do and be more.

To Henry, Joseph and Xavier, for your ready smiles, your delight in my presence and your imaginations. Thank you for inspiring me to look for the learning and fun in all we do.

To Michael, Megan and Hugh, for being wonderful siblings, for your friendship and wit and for keeping it real.

To all of my friends, past and present; for the inspiration, the laughs and the challenges, and for being part of my life.

To the writers and directors, cast and crew of the *West Wing* and *NCIS* for the entertainment and diversion.

To the makers of Illy Coffee and cocoa growers everywhere, thank you, thank you, thank you.

To everyone at Matador for helping turn this dream into a reality.